Getting to Grips with Asperger Syndrome

Getting to Grips with Asperger Syndrome

Understanding Adults on the Autism Spectrum

Carol Hagland

Jessica Kingsley Publishers
London and Philadelphia

First published in 2010
by Jessica Kingsley Publishers
116 Pentonville Road
London N1 9JB, UK
and
400 Market Street, Suite 400
Philadelphia, PA 19106, USA

www.jkp.com

Library of Congress Cataloging in Publication Data
Hagland, Carol.
  Getting to grips with Asperger syndrome : understanding adults on the autism spectrum
/ Carol Hagland.
    p. cm.
  Includes bibliographical references and index.
  ISBN 978-1-84310-977-8 (pb : alk. paper) 1. Asperger's syndrome. 2. Autism spectrum
disorders. I. Title.
  RC553.A88H34 2009
  616.85'8832--dc22

                                                    2009010544

British Library Cataloguing in Publication Data
A CIP catalogue record for this book is available from the British Library

ISBN 978 1 84310 977 8

Printed and bound in Great Britain by
MPG Books Limited, Cornwall

Contents

Introduction

This book has been written as a result of approximately fifteen years' experience of working with adults with Asperger syndrome in different settings. One of the overriding impressions from all this work has been how little the condition is understood. Although it has been a recognized condition for over sixty years, and many people know the name, few really understand what it means for those who have the condition and for those who help to care for them. In residential and supported living settings, most of the people who are caring for those with Asperger syndrome have little understanding of what the diagnosis really means, and this makes it very difficult for them to offer useful support.

Many of the people that I have worked with have not been diagnosed until relatively late in life, some even into their fifties and sixties. These people have often lived with bullying, teasing, ridicule, suspicion and downright hostility from those around them for many years, and as a result find it difficult to trust anyone new. They often worry that they are going mad, or are monsters, because they are made aware every day of how different they are from most people. For many, especially those with little family support, every day can be a battle.

The aim of this book is to describe Asperger syndrome in a straightforward way that can be understood by anyone.

Each of the areas of difference that can cause problems is examined, and suggestions are made as to how problems might be tackled if they arise. Many people with Asperger syndrome become known to social and health services only when they are in crisis: relationships have broken down, or the person has lost a job, or been evicted from their home. Sometimes this crisis will have triggered a mental health problem, typically depression. Often it seems that if only the person could have received more help and understanding earlier in the sequence of events, the crisis might have been avoided. It is my aim in writing this book to aid that understanding, and perhaps even prevent a few of these crises.

The brief case illustrations do not reflect known individuals, but are compiled from a range of observations by myself and my former colleagues. They have been chosen to represent the kinds of experiences and problems that people with Asperger syndrome may have.

There are no academic references included in the text, but a list of useful further reading is given at the end. Whether you are the person with Asperger syndrome, a parent, a relative or a professional person involved in the care of someone with Asperger syndrome, I hope that you will find something of interest and help in these pages.

Chapter 1

What is Asperger Syndrome?

Asperger (or Asperger's) syndrome has become increasingly well known over the last twenty years or so. There have been a large number of books written about it, both from the position of someone who has been diagnosed with the condition, and from that of someone who has to care for them. Many of these books look at the effects of Asperger syndrome (AS) in children, and suggest ways to help and manage them. The difficulties of children with AS are being recognized, and a diagnosis made, much sooner than was the case even ten years ago, and this can be extremely helpful for both the child and the parents, although resources are still very limited. Despite the limited resources, this increased rate of diagnosis does tend to mean that at least the child's difficulties are recognized and understood earlier and better by the family and, it is hoped, by the school as well. Ideally, such a diagnosis will lead to special arrangements being made to support the child's education and social functioning.

A generation ago, Asperger syndrome was much less well known, and this kind of specialist support was unlikely to be available at all. Consequently, there are still many adults in society who have AS but who have never been diagnosed, or have received their diagnosis late in life. They will often have struggled through childhood and adolescence feeling alienated and misunderstood, and those around them will have remained frustrated and perplexed. Difficulties that could perhaps have been minimized if the condition had been recognized earlier are more likely to have become entrenched problems. This book is aimed primarily at those adults and the people who support them.

Maybe you are a person with AS who has just received a diagnosis, or a family member or carer who suspects that someone you help may have the condition. This book is intended to help you understand Asperger syndrome, and make sense of what may sometimes seem irrational behaviour. It will also suggest avenues to explore if you wish to confirm a suspected diagnosis.

Usually adults with AS will have always appeared odd or eccentric to others, and some of those less fortunate may have been diagnosed wrongly with other conditions. Many of them will still be struggling. The book aims to describe the kinds of difficulties that people with AS can experience, and to suggest ways that those around them can help. It also aims to help those who are struggling to support someone with AS to find alternative ways of coping. This may be a partner, family member, paid carer or other professional.

Defining Asperger syndrome

Before we begin, we need to define what we mean by Asperger syndrome. Many people have heard the name, and think that they know a little about it. However, often people are unclear about what it means to have Asperger syndrome. One of the most widely accepted sets of criteria used to define Asperger syndrome is that of Gillberg and Gillberg (1989; see Further

Reading). They suggest that in order to qualify for a diagnosis the person must have:

Social problems (at least two of the following):

- difficulties interacting with peers
- indifference to peer contacts
- difficulties interpreting social cues
- socially and emotionally inappropriate behaviours.

Narrow interest (at least one of the following):

- exclusion of other activities
- repetition
- learning by heart rather than understanding meaning.

Repetitive routines (at least one of the following):

- routines which affect every aspect of everyday life
- routines which affect others.

Odd speech and language (at least three of the following):

- delayed development
- superficially perfect expressive language
- formal pedantic language
- odd prosody, peculiar voice characteristics
- impairment of comprehension including misinterpretations of literal or implied meanings.

Non-verbal communication problems:

- limited use of gestures
- clumsy or gauche body language
- limited facial expression

- inappropriate facial expression
- peculiar stiff gaze.

Motor clumsiness:

- poor performance on neurodevelopmental tests.

What do these differences look like in practice? If it is possible to describe a 'typical' person with Asperger syndrome, then they will probably look something like the following:

- often male, although more and more females are being diagnosed

- has an all-consuming interest, often in something unusual or obscure, about which they will talk at length and in great detail, frequently boring or alienating those around them

- socially isolated, with few friends of either sex and rarely any sexual partners

- often seen as selfish, self-centred or thoughtless by those close to them

- strongly dislikes and resists change, getting upset out of all proportion

- may interrupt others' conversations, change the subject abruptly or seem not to listen

- may talk in an oddly formal, almost stilted fashion, often too loudly

- fails to pick up hints or cues in social situations

- says or does the wrong thing, to the embarrassment of others

- poor at dealing with personal hygiene, domestic chores and other regular demands

- may have an explosive temper or temper tantrums

- worries about all kinds of things, often quite small things

- poor at dealing with money and paying bills

- may have odd dislikes around food or clothing.

As noted above, people with Asperger syndrome will often have seemed odd or unusual for most of their life. Typically, they have great difficulty making friends, or if they do make friends, they do not manage to keep them. They tend to say or do the wrong thing at the wrong time, which annoys or embarrasses those around them, yet at the same time they can often appear unaware of having caused a problem.

Sometimes, though, especially as adults, they have the opposite problem, in that they have learned that they often get things wrong and, as a result, have become super-anxious about saying or doing the wrong thing. This can make the person with AS withdraw completely from social interaction, and be very wary of anyone new. Sometimes, people with AS can become quite angry with the rest of the world, because they feel so misunderstood.

People with AS often have great problems with close relationships, either failing completely to find a partner or, having found someone, behaving in such a way that the partner eventually gives up and withdraws, hurt and puzzled. Sadly the person with Asperger syndrome will usually also be hurt and puzzled, having no idea where they went wrong. Of course, this can happen in any close relationship, but for someone with Asperger syndrome there is often a long history of having either no relationships or many failed relationships, to a much greater extent than for most of us.

This difficulty with relationships generally will be mirrored by related problems around getting and keeping a job, and being able to live independently. In part, some of these problems will also be the result of interpersonal difficulties, such as falling out with the boss or the landlady, but they can be the result of practical problems such as being able to organize what has to be done at work, or remembering to pay the rent, or to keep their surroundings clean. In the job market, many people with AS will either have failed to get a job at all or, where they have succeeded, they will often quickly have lost their job again, for reasons of unpunctuality, forgetfulness or the breakdown of relationships with colleagues and supervisors. Not uncommonly, the person with Asperger syndrome will have strong opinions as to how a job should be done, and can become difficult or aggressive with those who wish to do things differently. This need to control things often has its roots in anxiety and the need to keep their environment the same. This is also related to the fact that those with Asperger syndrome like rules. Once they have established a set of rules for a given situation, they are very reluctant to change these rules, or deviate from them. They find it hard to be flexible, and may try to insist that others do what they want too.

Anxiety is a major symptom of Asperger syndrome. Those with the condition worry about all kinds of things, especially when they are faced with something new, or things have to change. Anxiety affects many parts of their lives, and is the root of their apparently obsessional behaviours and rigidity with routines. Any kind of change provokes additional anxiety, making people with AS very sensitive to change. While many of us dislike change, for people with AS change feels very threatening and they will go to great lengths to resist it. Sometimes anxiety can cause the person with AS to lose a job, because they are simply overwhelmed by coping with the demands of a new job, new people and a new place all at once.

In order to cope with their anxiety, many people with AS seek to control and maintain their environment as best they can. They like everything to remain the same. This need for sameness can also result in lots of anxious, repetitive questioning of those around them, which others find very frustrating, but which is intended to seek reassurance. Rather than other people giving reassurance, what often happens is that they get angry, so the situation escalates. Extreme anxiety can lead to aggressive or violent outbursts which result in the person being seen as, at best, unpredictable or, at worst, violent and dangerous.

The key symptom that defines those with AS, however, is their difficulty in making sense of other people. They find it hard to understand all the subtle social rules by which most of us operate, and are very poor at reading non-verbal or emotional signals from other people. They can often act in ways that seem unfeeling or even antisocial to those around them, simply because they do not understand how things look from someone else's point of view. This ability to put yourself 'in someone else's shoes' is what is often referred to as having a 'theory of mind'. Most of us have the ability to at least guess what someone else might think or feel in a given situation. People with AS find this extraordinarily difficult. As a result they may seem thoughtless, and even unkind, to others. Alternatively, they can often appear somewhat naïve and childlike in the style of their social interactions. While this can be quite endearing at times, it can also be puzzling and very frustrating for someone who is trying to interact with a person who appears at first sight to be a reasonably able adult, but who does not always behave like one.

Some people who have already been diagnosed with Asperger syndrome feel that the problem does not lie with them, but with the rest of the world around them. While they may have a point, nevertheless they have to live in the world that the rest of us inhabit, and we have to be able to cope with their differences. The aim of this book is to make both of these easier. As with any human relationship, if we understand each other, life becomes much less complicated.

We shall now move on to a brief history of the condition, and look at how it is currently diagnosed. If you or your family member has already received a diagnosis, you may want to skip this part and go on to look in more detail at the difficulties that the condition can present, and how you may be able to help to minimize these. However, for those who are paid carers, the discussions about diagnosis, in this chapter and the next, may help you to understand why someone has been given the label of AS, and how this differs from other conditions which might, at first sight, look similar.

Background

Asperger syndrome was first identified in 1944, by Hans Asperger, who labelled it 'autistic psychopathy'. His original paper described four young men that he had seen professionally, who appeared to have a number of characteristics in common. These were:

- a pattern of unusual, obsessive interests
- unusual speech although not delayed developmentally
- social difficulties
- physical awkwardness or clumsiness
- some difficult or antisocial behaviours.

However, despite this early description of the syndrome, the condition was not widely known or recognized until 1981, when Lorna Wing began to investigate it further. She dropped the label 'autistic psychopathy' that Asperger had used, because she felt this carried derogatory overtones, and coined the term 'Asperger syndrome'.

In his descriptions, Asperger felt that antisocial behaviour was a significant part of the syndrome, but Lorna Wing did not agree. However, both Lorna Wing and Hans Asperger felt that AS was a form of autism. Lorna Wing went on to develop the idea of the 'autistic spectrum' which she felt covered a range of related conditions. Since then there have been a number of attempts to define the condition satisfactorily, none of which has proved entirely successful. There is still some disagreement as to whether autism and AS are part of the same condition, or whether they are two separate ones. They have some characteristics in common, but there are some notable differences. Furthermore, the criteria which are used to define AS vary between different researchers, and it is still difficult to find a set of criteria which is accepted by all.

How is a diagnosis made?

While there are still some disagreements about which criteria are essential for a diagnosis, there is broad agreement in many areas. However, in most cases, the diagnosis must still be made by experienced clinicians who have considerable knowledge of the condition. They will often use a formal checklist of some kind to decide whether or not the condition is AS, although most of these checklists are designed for use with children, rather than adults. Some clinicians favour using neuropsychological tests also. An important part of the diagnostic process will be to talk to parents or others who knew the person when they were growing up. Information about early development is essential. It usually takes quite a long time to gather all the information needed to make a formal diagnosis, although with experience this does become easier.

One of the difficulties in arriving at a universal definition of Asperger syndrome is its variety. Although there are a number of criteria which are now widely accepted as diagnostic, any one individual with AS can be very different from another. Indeed there are theoretically over one hundred thousand possible combinations of symptoms which could lead to a diagnosis of the condition. For those who are not familiar with the condition, this can be confusing. Even more confusing is the fact that, over the years, different people have come up with slightly different sets of criteria for diagnosis, because of the disagreements which exist. This makes it very difficult for those who are not familiar with the condition to feel confident about their diagnosis.

What adds to the difficulty is that other conditions can look like AS to the inexperienced. As stated above, it is very important to have information about the person's development from childhood to adulthood to be able to make a reliable diagnosis. AS is a developmental condition, which means that it is present from birth and is the result of biological differences in the person's brain. Consequently, if the problems have not been present since early childhood, then the person does not have AS.

What causes Asperger syndrome?

The cause of the differences in brain development and function is uncertain, but there is evidence that they may be at least partly genetic, as the condition often seems to run in families. Even where parents do not have all the characteristics necessary for a formal diagnosis, there are frequently recognizable signs of AS in their characters. There is also evidence that children with AS have a greater than average number of engineers in their family tree. As a result, it has been suggested that Asperger syndrome is simply an extreme form of the male brain. It has been shown that women who have higher levels of male hormone in their blood during pregnancy are more likely to have an autistic child, and this may be relevant to AS too. The idea is that typical male brains are driven to generate systems, and understand the causes of things, while typical female brains are more concerned with how others are thinking and feeling. There are exceptions of course, and some men and some women will have the other sex's predominant style of thinking, while most people have a mixture of both.

Although there is clearly a genetic component to AS, there is also some evidence that mild brain injury around birth can produce AS. Parents will often report that the person with AS had a difficult birth, with the mother having had a long and difficult labour. Some children with AS will have been born early, and some rather late, that is, outside of the normal forty weeks gestation period. There is, however, no obvious pattern to the kinds of birth difficulties that produce AS, although it is evident that anything unusual in the birth process increases the risk.

What is clear is that AS is *not* the result of poor parenting. Parents often worry that they have somehow caused the problems, and in the early years, when the condition was first identified, there was a suggestion that both AS and autism might be the result of cold or inadequate parenting. This has now been completely discounted. There are differences in the brains of those with AS and those without, which have been identified on brain scans, so it is clearly a biologically based condition.

It is also possible that a number of different causes may all lead to a similar pattern of difficulties which come to be labelled as AS. In other words, there is not just one cause. At present we do not know the whole truth. However, what does seem to happen is that the person's difficulties colour their early life and learning, and affect the development of both personality and intellect. There is no doubt that early intervention and specialist teaching can help enormously to contain these difficulties, and make them more manageable. In recent years there has been an improvement in both diagnosis and educational provision for children with AS. While this is a step forward, there is still a long way to go before services really meet the needs of children with AS. For adults, services are almost non-existent in most areas of the UK.

Where people have reached adulthood without this understanding and additional help, they can have significantly greater problems in fitting into society, and as a consequence may develop mental health problems in addition to AS. Indeed, it is often these mental health problems that bring the person to the notice of health and social services. At this point they may finally receive a diagnosis of AS in addition to their mental health diagnosis. However, many mental health services do not understand or even recognize AS, and it is not uncommon for people to be given the wrong diagnosis. Even if a correct diagnosis of AS has been given, there is still a dearth of services for adults with AS, unless they also have a mild learning disability. Diagnosis may give families some explanation of a person's problems, but it does not necessarily open the door to further help.

Relationship to autism

As already noted, there is still considerable debate about whether AS is a form of autism or not. Some clinicians feel strongly that it is, because there are a number of similarities, while others feel that it is sufficiently different from autism to be considered as a separate condition. It has been suggested that AS is the form that autism takes in the more intellectually able while, traditionally, autism proper is more often associated with intellectual impairment. While there is certainly an association between intellectual impairment and autism, the existence of a unidimensional spectrum, as suggested by Lorna Wing, remains uncertain. It is possible to find people with autism who are of normal ability, as well as people with Asperger syndrome who have some degree of intellectual impairment.

Further disagreements centre around whether either the antisocial elements identified by Hans Asperger or the obsessional interests need always be present for a diagnosis. Certainly, much of what gets labelled 'antisocial behaviour' actually arises out of the difficulties that the person with AS has in understanding social rules and expectations. The 'offences' that they appear to commit often arise out of social incompetence rather than malicious intent.

Both autism and AS still appear to be more frequently identified amongst males. However, in recent years more girls and women are being diagnosed with AS, and it has become apparent that the presentation of AS in women can be somewhat different from that in men. The obsessional interests may be less obvious, and may show themselves in patterns of behaviour such as collecting dolls or soft toys, in eating disorders, or in obsessional behaviours around health or personal hygiene, which are less obviously unusual. In addition, some clinicians believe that women with AS tend to be more sociable than men with the condition, which may also make it less obvious.

What are the similarities between AS and autism?

The following characteristics are common to both conditions:

- an abnormal social presentation
- difficulty forming friendships
- some abnormality of speech

- obsessional/repetitive behaviours

- poor motor co-ordination, or odd movements

- difficulties with non-verbal communication and/or emotional perception

- over-sensitive to light, noise, textures, etc.

What are the differences?

In Asperger syndrome, the following characteristics are apparent:

- pedantic, formal and often repetitive language style, with often unusual intonation

- some abnormalities in language development, but less marked than in autism

- poor comprehension, with a tendency to take things literally

- normal or near-normal level of ability

- can be very knowledgeable about their area of special interest

- some interest in social interaction, even though they have difficulties with it

- can be passive and lack initiative.

On the other hand, those with autism are usually much less interested in other people, except to get them to meet their needs. Their difficulties are much more obvious from very early in life (eighteen months to three years). In addition autism is more frequently associated with:

- a history of significant language delay in childhood, with often limited language in adulthood

- learning disability or intellectual impairment
- earlier diagnosis, probably because language and social impairments are more obvious
- marked social withdrawal, usually apparent from early childhood
- repetitive, often self-stimulatory behaviours (tapping, spinning objects, repetitive sounds).

Does diagnosis matter?

At one level, the answer to this is no. If someone comes with a problem which can be helped, and that help is given, it does not really matter what label the problem is given. Indeed some people who come for help do not want to be labelled and will resent attempts to do so. This is entirely understandable, and should be respected. However, unfortunately, the reality is that to get the help and services that the person needs, a diagnostic label is usually necessary. This is particularly the case with educational provision for children, but it is equally true for any form of funding, residential care or other specialist provision.

For adults, getting help can be even more difficult. Both health and social services in most areas are severely short of cash, and thus services are restricted to those who are considered in most need. In many areas, a diagnosis of AS alone will not be enough to get the person the help that they and their families often feel they need, because the disorder will not be considered sufficiently disabling.

Psychiatrists, as doctors, spend much of their time attempting to refine diagnoses, because they feel that it is helpful to be able to categorize a person's difficulties. This can then enable them to develop a particular kind of drug treatment which fits that category. This model of treatment is sometimes called the 'medical model'. In brief, it means that any mental disorder is seen in the same light as a physical illness, in that it has specific symptoms which can then be treated in a specific way, usually with drugs. Unfortunately, many mental disorders, and particularly the developmental disorders, do not fit into neatly defined categories. Some conditions can exist together, and some appear to be very similar to each other.

Psychologists tend to take a different approach to both mental illness and other kinds of mental disorder, often feeling that it is more helpful to look at the kinds of difficulties that people experience, and try to find ways to help them deal with those. In this situation, the label can be less important, at least to the psychologist.

Seeking help

Many people with AS come to mental health services as adults, not knowing what their particular problem is, except that they have been struggling for years to fit in. Usually they come for help because they have come to a crisis point in their lives. An elderly parent who was providing support may have died, or a partner who was formerly supportive may have decided to leave. Sometimes the person themselves will have suffered a loss of home or job for some other reason, and the consequent difficulties have led them to become anxious and depressed. At worst, the person may have become psychotic, and had to be hospitalized for treatment.

In these situations it often becomes gradually apparent that the immediate problems described by the person are only the tip of the iceberg, and that they have actually been having difficulties in coping with life for years. It may not always be obvious at first that these difficulties can be explained by a diagnosis of AS, but by a gradual process of elimination of other possible conditions it may become apparent that this is the most likely explanation.

However, there are a range of other conditions which can appear similar to AS in some ways. Usually it is only possible to be certain of the diagnosis if the professional can make contact with family members who have known the person since childhood. Sometimes this is not possible, either because such people are no longer alive, or accessible, or sometimes because the person themselves is unwilling for them to be consulted. In this situation, it is impossible to give a firm or reliable diagnosis.

Getting a diagnosis

It may be that you have suspected for some time that you, your family member, child, partner or person you look after has AS. There has been much more publicity of the condition in recent years, with films, books and television programmes devoted to it, and as a result many people have come to believe that this is the explanation for the difficulties that they experience themselves, or that they see in a particular person. If this is your experience, you may be wondering how you can go about getting your suspicions confirmed.

The first port of call should be the family doctor. However, if your concern is for someone else, you may find that you cannot persuade the person to attend with you. If not, then for reasons of confidentiality it will be very difficult to go any further. The doctor cannot make a referral without the consent of the person concerned, unless they are a child. However, you may be able to discuss the difficulties generally with the doctor, who may be able to suggest other contacts.

To obtain a proper diagnosis, you need to persuade the person to attend the doctor with you, and to agree that they can be referred to the local mental health services. It is likely that you will have to do this before you can access more specialist help. They will make an initial assessment and should then refer you on to someone who has more knowledge of the condition, and who should be able to make a proper diagnosis. Either you, or someone else who has known the person since early childhood, will need to provide information about their early development. The person who is being referred will need to agree to this information being given. If they do not, there is little more that can be done. Frustrating as that may seem, unless the person is deemed to be legally incapable of looking after their affairs, you cannot act without their consent.

Often what happens, as we have already noted, is that the person with AS will have hit some kind of crisis which has provoked the need to try to define what is wrong. A crisis like this may make the person more amenable to seeking help than they may previously have been.

If there is no obvious centre of expertise or person who is willing and able to diagnose in your area, then you may need to consider the privately funded option. In this case, you may have to pay for an assessment leading to a diagnosis. The best place to start is the National Autistic Society, who have many contacts and sources of free advice to offer. Even if you have already arranged a private consultation, it is still worth contacting the National Autistic Society to gain more information about the condition. Despite their name, they do also have considerable expertise in the area of Asperger syndrome.

What to do with a diagnosis of AS

Maybe you have already had a diagnosis of AS confirmed, and are wondering where to go from here. Unfortunately, in many areas, the diagnosis will not actually help you to get any additional services, nor will it open any doors to help from social services. There are several reasons for this. First, people with

AS, although being identified more frequently than in the past, are still relatively uncommon in the population. As a result, many professionals have little experience of their difficulties, or training in how to help. Second, where specialist services have been set up, these are usually the result of short-term initiatives and special grant monies. Once the funding ends, the services often disappear. Those that remain are too often only diagnostic services, with no social services or other support services linked to them. Third, money is in short supply in both health and social services, and, in some areas of the UK, you will literally have to be on the brink of sleeping on the street before any help will be forthcoming. Most people with AS are managing to get by, albeit with difficulty, and have help from family members, even though those family members are often struggling to cope. Consequently they are not seen as being needy enough.

So what's the point, you may ask, of getting a diagnosis, if it does not assist you in getting further help or financial support? What it *will* do is give both you and the person with AS a model to explain the problems that they will have had all their life. Often this can be a huge relief. There will have been a sense for many years that 'something is wrong' without any real explanation for why this should be so. The person with AS may have struggled along, failing in education, failing at work and failing in relationships, yet not understanding why. Families and carers may have wondered why someone who might appear very able in some ways can fail to remember to do simple things like paying a bill or putting the rubbish out. A diagnosis of AS can explain why, and, once the condition is fully understood, can open the way to more realistic and tailored help.

This can be empowering to those who are trying to offer help and support, whether family, partners, friends or paid carers, because they can begin to reinterpret what the person with AS is doing. Their behaviour will no longer be seen as just weird, irritating or sometimes downright challenging. Once you can understand why someone acts the way they do, the behaviour becomes much easier to tolerate and deal with. If you also have ideas as to how to minimize the difficulties that the person with AS is experiencing, you can gradually work towards developing an easier and less stressful life for you both.

We have seen that Asperger syndrome has its roots in differences in the make-up of the brain. These differences make it hard for someone with AS to fit into the world that the rest of us inhabit. We operate by a number of unwritten, and usually unspoken, social rules, which most of us pick up as we go along. People with AS do not seem to be able to do this. One very able young man that I worked with some years ago commented, 'I watch other people interact with each other, and I can see they are doing something which I can't do, and don't understand.' This was remarkably perceptive, but sadly he still struggled in social situations.

The parts of the brain which enable us to pick up and learn these social rules do not work as well as they should for people with AS. These parts of the brain deal with attention, concentration, immediate memory, planning, organizing, and following sequences such as instructions or conversations. They also help us to monitor and make use of feedback, both from our practical experiences and from our dealings with other people. Thus they are very important to enable us to cope with both the complexities of modern life and the complexities of social situations.

In the remainder of this book we shall examine the areas of life which most often present problems to people with AS and their families or carers, and look at ways in which these can be managed so that problems are minimized, as far as is possible. However, it is important to realize that Asperger syndrome cannot be cured. The problems will not simply go away, whatever you do. Nevertheless, in understanding where the difficulties arise, and finding ways in which they can be helped, many problems can be avoided.

In the next chapter we shall briefly look at some of the other conditions that may mimic AS or be confused with it. By careful observation, you may find that you can eliminate some of these as possible explanations of the difficulties you encounter. Or you may realize that one of these alternatives offers a better explanation of the person's difficulties than AS appears to do. This may set you on the road to helping that person more effectively.

SUMMARY

o   Asperger syndrome is defined by a range of criteria, although there is still some disagreement as to which of these are most important.

o   Asperger syndrome is the result of differences in brain development, and is not caused by poor parenting.

o   Asperger syndrome is similar to autism in some ways, but there are important differences.

o   Asperger syndrome in adults may be more difficult to diagnose because of the difficulty in getting reliable information about the person's early life.

o   At present, a diagnosis will not necessarily ensure access to appropriate services, but it does help the person and their family understand the cause of their difficulties.

o   Diagnosis will require access to specialist services, which can be done either through the family doctor or by seeking a private consultation.

Chapter 2

Differential Diagnosis

We have looked at how Asperger syndrome can be difficult to diagnose, especially in adults, but a further complication is that it can be difficult to distinguish from a number of other conditions.

Developmental disorders

There are several other developmental disorders which can appear similar to AS. A developmental disorder is one which shows itself in early childhood, and appears to have a biological basis, rather than being the result of particular experiences. These appear to be rooted, like AS, in differences in the way the brain develops. It is not certain what causes these conditions, but it is likely that they are caused either by minor brain injury that happens around the time of birth or by genetic differences.

In some cases, developmental disorders appear to run in families, which suggests a possible genetic component, but, as with Asperger syndrome, our knowledge of these other developmental conditions is not sufficiently detailed to enable us to be certain. What is certain is that the difficulties appear early in life, and when the child goes to school it will rapidly become clear that there are, or have been, problems of learning, development and/or management.

We know that all children with AS have some difficulties with social interaction and language. They also have problems with memory and learning. Often there seem to be behavioural problems as well. All of the other developmental disorders can result in a range of problems in these areas too, but each will be slightly different. However, none of them is very clearly defined, and there may be areas of overlap.

These other developmental disorders are listed below:

- ADHD/ADD

- pathological demand avoidance syndrome

- PDD-NOS

- semantic-pragmatic disorder

- Tourette's syndrome.

In the early stages of diagnosis, especially with children, these various conditions may also be examined as possible explanations for any unusual patterns of behaviour the child is demonstrating. Often these other diagnoses will need to be eliminated before a diagnosis of AS is made. The differentiation of the conditions is complex, and the help of a psychiatrist will be needed. Careful observation and questioning of the parents and teachers will also be needed to determine the correct diagnosis.

In adults, diagnosis of developmental disorders is even more difficult, because later experiences will have affected the person's development too. Furthermore, most of these developmental disorders have been defined relatively recently, and it is not yet certain how they will show themselves in adults. However, in brief the differences are as follows.

ADHD or ADD

These initials stand for attention deficit hyperactivity disorder, or attention deficit disorder. ADHD is probably the second most widely known developmental disorder, after AS. ADD is another form of ADHD where the person still has difficulty in concentrating, but this is not associated with the high levels of activity seen in ADHD. People with these disorders share the problems of concentration that are often seen in people with AS, but they are more socially aware, and their major problem is that of being distractible and unable to settle to anything. They find busy, noisy environments difficult because they have great difficulty in shutting out unwanted stimulation, so they may become more and more agitated. This can be a particular problem for children when they are in a mainstream school, where there is much noise and bustle, and a lot going on around them. Such children fail to learn because they cannot focus on what they are trying to do. They may wish to be sociable but their behaviours tend to alienate others, as they tend to be constantly restless or active. Their language development and usage, however, is usually normal. The problems may improve somewhat as the child gets older, but do not disappear.

Pathological demand avoidance syndrome

There is some disagreement as to the robustness of this as a diagnostic group, but it has been suggested that there is a particular group of children who are extremely disturbed by any demand being made upon them and will, as a result, go to abnormal lengths to avoid complying. Unlike many developmental disorders, the sex ratio is about equal. These children are described as socially manipulative in avoiding demands and may also be aggressive. Such children do have a theory of mind, and an awareness of how their behaviour affects others, but they are said to have no shame or pride. They may suffer panic attacks. This condition has only been identified in children so far, and if it does exist as a distinct diagnostic group, it is not certain how it will be demonstrated in an adult form.

PDD-NOS

These initials stand for pervasive developmental disorder not otherwise specified, and this title, perhaps more than any other, demonstrates how difficult it can be to define some of these developmental conditions. This has been described as a milder form of autism, with some language difficulties, but fewer stereotyped behaviours. It may also be called 'atypical autism'. As children, it is clear that they are not developing normally, but the pattern of their difficulties is not as clearly identifiable as any of the other conditions. There may be problems of poor language development, and some withdrawal from social situations, but these are not as marked as in true autism.

Semantic-pragmatic disorder

This is a disorder of language development which makes it difficult for the person to understand the subtleties of social interaction. Their language tends to remain immature and concrete, but without obvious abnormalities. Non-verbal communication is normal, and in other ways these people tend to be more socially skilled than those with AS, and are more aware of the impact of their behaviour on others. However, they will have difficulties with the more subtle and emotional aspects of social interaction. They will also often find it very difficult to express what they are feeling verbally.

Tourette's syndrome

This syndrome is characterized by the presence of 'tics' or repetitive pieces of behaviour. These can be physical, as in muscular tics or patterns of movement, or verbal, as in repetitive swearing or rehearsal of a particular word or phrase. These can look superficially like some of the rituals and routines seen in AS, but these routines are not motivated by a need to maintain stability in the person's environment, and they do not give any comfort to the person concerned, as they do in AS. Indeed, the person with Tourette's syndrome will feel that the behaviour is beyond their control for much of the time. Tourette's syndrome can manifest itself in a variety of ways, but again the sufferers are usually aware of the impact of their behaviour on others to a much greater degree. For a firm diagnosis, the person must have multiple motor tics and at least one verbal tic present over a significant period of time. Their language development is normal. However, a further complication is that on occasions people with AS may also have Tourette's syndrome.

When, as a clinician, you meet with an adult who wants to know what is wrong with them, trying to diagnose any developmental disorder in retrospect is not easy. As already noted, most of these adults who present themselves to adult mental health services have never received any diagnosis, and they and their families are simply aware that they have some problems, which they have had for many years.

The picture may be further complicated by the onset of mental illness, in addition to whatever other problems the person may have had before. When a clinician is trying to understand the overall picture, and make a diagnosis, the existence of more than one condition can be confusing, and it is often very difficult to get enough information to give a confident answer. This can be frustrating for both the sufferer and his or her family, who may have come to seek help and hope to find out exactly 'what is wrong'.

Mental disorders

There are a number of other conditions and disorders that have a later age of onset, which can look like AS in an adult. When someone new first comes for help, it can be difficult to decide exactly what is wrong with them, especially if, as already noted, there is little information about how they were before. Those who work in mental health services are used to dealing with problems like depression and anxiety, and sometimes with more serious problems such as schizophrenia or other psychotic illnesses. They may also encounter some people who have personality disorders. However, the person with a developmental disorder usually provides an additional challenge. While this person may come along with a form of mental disorder that is easily recognizable, they will also have other characteristics which are not, and the picture they present to the professionals will be confusing, unless the clinician concerned is familiar with developmental disorders too. In addition, some forms of mental disorder can resemble some developmental disorders, at least superficially, and for those who are not experienced in diagnosing these conditions, it can be difficult to be certain what is the correct label to give. In this next section, we shall look at those mental disorders which can appear similar to AS.

Schizophrenia

Schizophrenia is a form of psychosis, which is difficult to define adequately. Although it has now been diagnosed for many years, it apparently takes a variety of forms and so, in terms of predicting outcome or even suitable treatment, a diagnosis of schizophrenia is not always very helpful. Typically it is associated with an initial period of agitation and distress, usually accompanied by some odd ideas or hallucinations and some loss of contact with reality. Its peak age of onset is from mid-teens to mid-twenties, although other types are sometimes diagnosed for the first time in people of middle age.

Some people may have a single episode of illness, and then recover, and never have another. Often this episode will occur after a period of stress and seems to be a breakdown in the person's capacity to cope. More commonly a person will have more than one episode, often deteriorating steadily over their lifetime, in terms of their capacity to cope independently. Such people are often very sensitive to stress, and a new breakdown may be triggered by relatively lower levels of stress as time goes on.

Others may suffer a single episode of illness in their teenage years and never really recover fully from it. As they get older, this group of sufferers tend to become more passive, and less able to function independently. They show little interest in life, or social interaction, and may appear withdrawn for much of the time. They may neglect their personal hygiene and appearance. It is this group of people who are most likely to be confused with people with AS. However, the main difference here is that those who develop schizophrenia have usually appeared to be quite normal as children. They may have seemed a little quiet or shy, but otherwise their language and behaviour will not have been a cause for concern. Their families will usually report a sudden change during teenage years, followed by a worsening condition as time goes by. AS does not usually get worse, although it can seem to do so if the person with AS develops an additional mental illness.

Approximately a quarter of people with schizophrenia also suffer from obsessive-compulsive disorder, so that superficially these people can also look like those with Asperger syndrome. However, the main differences will be that people with AS will have had difficulties since early childhood, whereas schizophrenia will typically begin following a trigger episode, a period of stress, or after drug usage, and its onset is likely to be in the teenage years or later. In addition, many people with schizophrenia will report having, or having had at some time, hallucinations. Typically the person will report hearing voices, which may be insulting, or may tell him or her to do things. More rarely they will see things which are not there, or get fixed ideas about being watched or followed.

People with AS will not have experiences like this, unless of course they also have this type of mental disorder. People with AS may talk to themselves, but if you listen carefully you will find that they are usually reminding themselves what they need to do. People who are schizophrenic and who talk to themselves are usually talking to their voices, and what you will hear is more like one side of a conversation, if it makes any sense at all. Often they will get quite agitated. Of course, in these days of mobile phones and earpieces, they may simply be talking to a friend! Careful observations and questioning, and carefully collected information about early life, will be essential to decide which is the correct diagnosis.

Obsessive-compulsive disorder (OCD)

Obsessive-compulsive disorder is a mental disorder where the sufferer feels driven to carry out often senseless routines to avoid disaster. Sometimes these rituals are simple but time consuming, such as having to touch every lamp-post as the person walks down a street. Other rituals involve checking things such as light switches, locks or the cleanliness of the environment. Obsessive-compulsive rituals and routines around housework are fairly common, and the person will feel driven to clean to a level of perfection that is way beyond normal. A stranger coming into the home may trigger off another bout of compulsive cleaning, even if the first round of cleaning has just been completed. Another common form is obsessive hand-washing, which can become so extreme that the person damages their skin and actually suffers from infections because they have disturbed the normal chemical balance of the skin. Other people can show obsessive teeth-cleaning, even to the point of wearing away the enamel on their teeth.

Typically these behaviours are driven by irrational beliefs about the risks of infection or contamination, or a belief that some kind of disaster will befall the sufferer, or his or her family members, if these rituals are not carried out. The repetitive actions are called 'compulsions' and the repetitive thoughts which drive them are called 'obsessions'. Hence the name 'obsessive-compulsive' disorder. The sufferer does not feel in control of these behaviours or the thoughts that drive them. In contrast, the so-called 'obsessions' of those with AS are much more likely to be all-consuming interests which are enjoyed, rather than fears that drive ritual behaviours.

People with AS are often referred to a psychologist for treatment of their 'obsessive-compulsive disorder' because they are seen to like strict routines and rituals, and to become distressed if they cannot observe these. However, the motivation for the routines of those with AS is usually rather different from those with true obsessive-compulsive disorder. People with AS like routine because it makes them feel safe and makes the world around them seem more predictable. Although they may become very anxious and upset if prevented from carrying out their rituals and routines, they do not typically expect that anything dramatic or dangerous will happen. Their routines do, however, make them feel safe and in control, and they actively wish to continue with them. People with OCD are more likely to feel at the mercy of their obsessions and rituals, and experience them as being out of their own control.

It will take careful questioning to determine which is the correct diagnosis to make here, and, confusingly, it is also possible to have both conditions together. Do not, however, rush into assuming that because someone appears to have repetitive rituals and routines, they must have OCD. If you are concerned, then you may need to try to persuade them to seek professional help.

Personality disorder

A personality disorder is a different kind of mental disorder, which arises as a result of unsatisfactory or abusive experiences during childhood. Sometimes the parents of the person have been deliberately neglectful or abusive, or sometimes just inadequate. Mentally ill parents often produce children who go on to develop a personality disorder. Personality disorder is a result of abnormal experiences and results in abnormal development. Such problems are hard to help. However, in recent years new therapeutic approaches, such as dialectical behaviour therapy, have appeared, which do seem to help some people.

Two kinds of personality disorder can sometimes be confused with AS:

SCHIZOID PERSONALITY DISORDER

Typically, the person is withdrawn, or odd and solitary, and may behave in ways that are seen as antisocial. They tend to lack social skills and avoid others, often appearing similar to adults with autism or AS. They also often appear detached from their surroundings. It has been suggested by some that this disorder is the same as AS, and that the person who first described it was in fact describing AS in adults. Once again there is disagreement among professionals about this, which further illustrates how difficult it can be to categorize these disorders.

SCHIZOTYPAL PERSONALITY DISORDER

In this kind of personality disorder, the person will usually have strange or paranoid ideas of reference, i.e. believing that unrelated incidents have particular significance to events in your own life (e.g. 'The world is out to get me' or 'I am being watched by the CIA'), or other odd or magical beliefs. While often appearing superficially normal, people with this diagnosis can hold some very strange beliefs, which they will often reveal if carefully questioned.

In both these kinds of personality disorder, the person tends not to be very sociable, but their early language development is usually normal, and their speech and intonation are normal, even if the content is a little odd. In addition, people with personality disorders will not usually show the same concern with routines, or anxiety if faced with change. Nor will they usually have the pattern of obsessive interest in a particular topic like those with AS, except perhaps where it relates to their odd beliefs. The other distinguishing feature of the personality disorders is that they have a later age of onset than AS, usually not appearing until at least seven or eight years of age, and more usually in early adolescence.

Depression

Depression as a separate mental disorder can be difficult to distinguish from Asperger syndrome because adults with AS are also very prone to depression. This is often what brings them to the notice of mental health services. However, where individuals have depression without Asperger syndrome, early development will have been normal and there will not be a history of obsessional interests. In addition, there will usually have been some trigger event or situation accounting for the onset of depression. Indeed, most forms of mental illness will usually be of later onset (early teens onwards) and will often be associated with obvious stresses, such as loss of job, loss of partner, loss of parent, etc. People with AS can, of course, develop depression for all of these reasons, but will also have a history of ongoing difficulties which go back to early childhood.

Chronic anxiety

Anxiety is a common problem and it is sometimes difficult to say at what point generalized anxiety might be considered a clinical disorder. It is generally accepted that when a symptom becomes so pronounced that it interferes with everyday life, then it has become abnormal. So, for example, many people are scared of dogs, but if that fear stops someone from going out of the house, then it would be considered abnormal. This kind of anxiety is usually called a phobia. Chronic anxiety, however, is not usually focused on just one thing. The person may worry about a whole range of things in their life, and this can become so overwhelming that it stops them from living a normal life.

If, someone is chronically anxious, but does not show the other features associated with AS, such as the inability to see another person's point of view, or an overwhelming special interest, then it is unlikely that the person has AS. Nevertheless, for those with AS it is true to say that their anxiety almost always interferes with their everyday life, so one could argue that everyone with AS has chronic anxiety. Certainly, as a group, those with AS tend to be much more anxious than most people. Anxiety can be difficult to treat. Medication for anxiety is fraught with difficulty, because most drugs that have been used to treat chronic anxiety become addictive. Psychological approaches may prove more fruitful, and regular use of techniques such as relaxation may keep the anxiety levels of the person with AS at a manageable level. This will be discussed further in Chapter 8.

How is Asperger syndrome different?

In contrast to the mental disorders discussed above, AS, like the other developmental disorders, will be present from very early childhood (one to five years). However, AS will often only be noticed when the child starts school and begins to mix with other children. In some cases, it may not become apparent until the child is approaching adolescence. This is particularly true if the child is an only or first child, so that the parents are unfamiliar with normal patterns of development.

Autism, on the other hand, is usually diagnosed much earlier, largely because of the obvious and early avoidance of physical and social contact, and the poor development of language. It is unlikely that someone with autism could reach adulthood without coming to the attention of health or social services, unless the condition was very mild, while people with AS often used to be missed, and many may still be.

It is, however, important to understand that all these conditions are not exclusive. In other words, those with developmental disorders can still develop a mental illness, and it is not impossible to have more than one condition appearing together. People with personality disorders can often become depressed too. There is a tendency to look for a single explanation for someone's difficulties, while it is quite possible that they may have two or more conditions at the same time. People with AS can and do develop mental illnesses, and may even, in some circumstances, have a personality disorder as well.

Therefore, in order to be confident about any diagnosis that is made, it is important to have the diagnosis made by a clinician who is experienced with AS, and to gather as much information as possible both about the person's current situation and about their early life. Parents, siblings, aunts and uncles, and even neighbours may all be able to help. Old school records can sometimes be invaluable. The problem in recent times is that, with the emphasis on confidentiality of personal material, such records have often been destroyed. In addition, if the person refuses their consent to approach others in their life, it is difficult to proceed. The only exception might be when there is a legal case pending, or the person is deemed to be incapable of giving informed consent.

Some people with AS may not want to be labelled, and may resist attempts to categorize them. If this is the case, then their wishes should be respected, unless there are very good legal reasons for not doing so. A reliable and useful diagnosis can only be made with the consent and co-operation of the person who believes that they have AS, or is willing to accept that they might have.

Aids to making a diagnosis

It should be clear from the discussion above that, to distinguish between these various conditions in an adult, it is essential to have reliable information from someone who knew that person as a small child. However, when faced with an adult who is middle-aged or older, it is difficult to be certain how reliable the information given will be. Parents, if still alive, may look back and remember selectively, either to emphasize difficulties or to minimize them. Memory is notoriously unreliable, even in the most careful observer, so information needs ideally to be verified from more than once source. In the real world of clinical practice, this is often very hard to do. One simply has to make the best of what information is available. Some types of information can be particularly helpful however. Consider how diagnosis can be helped by the following different types of information that might be available:

A history of language development can be crucial in making the correct diagnosis. Autism is associated with significantly delayed development and limited language skills, while Asperger syndrome is associated with better early language development but unusual, over-formal use of language later on. However, it is worth noting that parents of those with AS often report that their first word is atypical, being something like 'aeroplane' rather than the more usual 'mummy' or 'daddy'.

Tourette's syndrome is characterized by the presence of tics which involve movement, but also verbal tics, which may include repetitive swearing. Other language development will usually be normal. Children with PDD-NOS, however, will show some delay in language development, but not the stereotyped behaviours common in autism, while those with semantic-pragmatic disorder will show slower language development, but their non-verbal and social communication will be normal.

The history of the person's social development is also very important, and parents and family members can often be very helpful in remembering how the person was as a growing child: whether they were able to make friends easily, who they played with, how they played and how they adjusted to going to school. Because children with AS can often appear superficially normal, especially in early childhood, it is often only when they start school that their difficulties become apparent. Siblings and parents will often have made allowances for odd behaviour and awkwardness, but unfortunately childhood peers tend not to be so tolerant. The child with AS will usually have found it hard to make friends at school, and will frequently have suffered a lot of bullying and teasing. Even teachers used to be remarkably insensitive in their dealings with such children when they were unaware of the condition. One would hope that this was not the case these days, with better knowledge of the condition. However, children with AS are often seen as unco-operative and difficult, even today, and this can make their time at school particularly problematic.

The obsessive interests of those with AS often bring them to the attention of others, either because they are seen as particularly clever or intelligent in relation to this topic, or because their interest is so relentless and all-consuming that they bore everyone around them by talking about it incessantly. Although the obsessive interest can be a vehicle for social contact and education, it can also be a barrier if the person with AS is allowed to develop their interest at the expense of everything else. If someone has an all-consuming interest like this, together with social difficulties, then a diagnosis of AS should be seriously considered.

Confirming the diagnosis

If, after considering all the alternatives above, you still feel sure that the person that you care for is likely to have Asperger syndrome, you may want to get this confirmed by a professional, and it may help to know how to seek out someone who could do this for you. If your local health services do not appear to have such a service, then it is worth contacting the National Autistic Society for advice and help. They also provide additional information that may be of help.

In the meantime, if you are convinced that a diagnosis of AS is the correct one, the following chapters may help you to understand and offer effective help and support. As with many conditions, understanding the nature of the problem can make it easier to cope. In each section, problem areas are described and then suggestions made as to how some of the resulting difficulties may be avoided or minimized.

SUMMARY

o   Asperger syndrome is a developmental disorder, which means that it is present from birth.

o   Asperger syndrome can be confused with other developmental disorders, but there are differences between them which can aid correct diagnosis.

o   Asperger syndrome in adults can also be confused with some forms of mental illness or personality disorder, but careful questioning, especially about early development, can often help to clarify the diagnosis.

o   Remember that it is possible for someone to have one or more of these other disorders, as well as Asperger syndrome.

o   In order to diagnose Asperger syndrome with any confidence, it is essential to have reliable information about the person's early development.

Chapter 3

Memory, Attention and Understanding

People with Asperger syndrome vary in ability as much as the rest of the population. Many are very bright, and some have become university professors. The majority, of course, will be of more average ability, and a few may have a mild learning disability. However, whatever their level of ability, all those with AS will have some problems with memory, attention and understanding. The extent of these problems will probably depend on their overall level of ability.

At best, the memory difficulties may take the form of simple absent-mindedness. The person may appear engrossed in another world, and while they can deal with complex and difficult problems in their chosen area of interest, they may not be able to remember to change their socks or have a bath! The more routine aspects of everyday life will often be neglected.

In others, the problems can be more severe. They may appear to listen to requests or instructions, but then completely fail to respond to these. This can happen despite many repeated requests. Sometimes they are unable to follow or remember what is said to them, unless sentences are kept very short and simple. In groups, where several people are talking together, they may opt out of the conversation altogether, and then join in unexpectedly with something quite unrelated.

This aspect of the condition can be infuriating for those who have to deal with it. It can seem as if the forgetting is deliberate. This is especially likely when the person with AS is very good at remembering things they are interested in, such as numbers, dates or types of railway engine. How, ask the family members or carers, can they remember such complicated things and yet forget simple tasks or requests?

> *Tony can remember the time and date of every visit made by his psychologist during the two years she has been seeing him, but when she visited him today he was unable to tell her what he did yesterday. How can this be? If he can remember all the details of her visits over the last two years, how can he claim to have forgotten something that happened only the day before?*

A bad memory or stubbornness?

Let's have a closer look at how memory works, as this may help to explain this apparent inconsistency. Memory is a complicated process, made up of several stages. Short-term memory relies on attention. In order to remember something, we have to attend to it, or concentrate on it, first. This process of attention then allows the information to be held in the conscious mind, so that the memory can register the important parts, thus allowing it to be recalled later. If the process of attention does not work very well, then the information is not registered or processed properly, and so cannot be remembered.

People with AS have problems with attention and concentration. They often find it hard to maintain their attention on anything for very long. Even with the things that interest them, they may only be able to attend for short periods at a time. They are often very distractible, and thus can easily lose track of what someone is saying to them, or forget what they are doing. If this happens after someone has spoken to them, then the information, request or instruction will not get into the memory properly, or at all. Thus they forget to do what is asked, and may even wander off and do something completely different.

> *Robin lives with his mother. They get on pretty well, but Robin's mother gets very cross with him at times. She says he does not listen when she asks him to do things, such as going into the next room to fetch something for her. Unfortunately she often chooses times when Robin is watching TV to ask him to do something. At these times, Robin is concentrating on the TV programme, and so does not really attend properly to his mother. Thus when he goes into the other room as she asks, he finds that he has forgotten what she said.*

But how is it that this same person can tell me which day of the week his birthday fell on for every year since he was born? Is that not memory? His memory for these kinds of things is far better than average, but he cannot remember what he was asked to fetch from the next room. That does not make any sense!

Actually it makes more sense than might appear at first. Information about dates, or birthdays, may be that person's special interest. We have already noted how common it is for people with AS to have a special interest. They will often be able to talk at length about this topic, boring everyone around them. They will go over and over the information that is of interest to them, perhaps in books or videos, reviewing it many times. By doing this, they are able to overcome their slowness of attention, and gradually the information will be learned and remembered. Because they are particularly interested, they go over the information repeatedly, and, as we all know, this is a good way to retain something that we want to remember. Thus they will appear to have an excellent memory for certain things, even if it may have taken them longer to learn the information than most people.

In addition, many people with AS are particularly good at numerical calculations, and, for example, working out the different days that a birthday will fall each year in the future, is a problem that they will be able to solve much more easily than most people.

Difficulties with understanding

People with AS often have problems with understanding or language comprehension. This is not usually about understanding individual words, but is related to their difficulty with attention and short-term memory described above. Long, complicated sentences confuse them, because they cannot hold all the information in their head long enough to make use of it. The result is that they forget what has been said to them, and thus fail to understand.

> *Ann has Asperger syndrome. She lives at home with her elderly mother, who has got used to Ann's ways and knows how to minimize the problems they have together. One day, Ann's older sister comes to stay. She has lived away from home for a number of years and has forgotten some of Ann's difficulties. She asks Ann, 'Can you go upstairs and get my coat for me? I need to get my purse because I am going to go down to the shops shortly. Is there anything you want? Or perhaps you would like to come with me?' Poor Ann is completely overwhelmed with words.*

She cannot remember and process everything her sister has said to her. She remembers the last bit and replies, 'Yes.' However, she makes no move to go upstairs for the coat, and her sister thinks she is just being awkward.

If you look closely at what Ann's sister has said, there are several parts to her communication. She wants Ann to go upstairs, she wants her to fetch the coat, she wants her purse from the coat pocket, she wants to go to the shops, and she asks if Ann wants anything and if she would like to go with her. There are six separate things here for Ann to remember and respond to, and it is hardly surprising that she cannot cope with them all. Ann's sister should have simply asked Ann if she could fetch her coat for her. Once that was achieved, she could then tell Ann that she was going to the shops, and ask if Ann would like to come too. If Ann refused, she might then ask if there was anything that she could get for her. The part about the purse is not important, and could be left out.

When you have to ask someone with AS to do something, or give them some instructions, it is important to bear this in mind. You are much more likely to succeed in getting your message across if you can keep things short and simple. Rather than using a long rambling sentence like Ann's sister did, break it down into several short ones, and let the person respond to each part before moving on to the next.

Difficulties with problem-solving

Poor short-term memory also contributes significantly to difficulties in problem-solving, simply because it is hard for the person with AS to hold information in their conscious mind long enough to manipulate information and come to a decision. Most of us do this without being aware that it is happening, but for those with AS it can be very challenging.

Consider what you do when you are trying to plan a day out. You need to think about where you are going, how you are going to get there, and the time that the journey will take. You also need to know what time you want to arrive at your destination, and thus be able to work backwards to know when you must leave home. You need to think about what time you have to be back home, and do a similar calculation to decide when you need to leave for the return journey. You will then need to consider if the time left will be enough to allow you to do what you want to do at your chosen place. Will the time available there be sufficient to make it a worthwhile visit? You may have a number of different things that you want to do or see while you are there, and these will also have to fit into your plan.

Most of us can work out a plan for a day out like this without too much difficulty. However, it does require holding a number of different pieces of information in your mind at once, and not losing sight of how these relate to each other. It is, in fact, quite a complex task, and is the kind of thing that someone with AS might find particularly difficult.

One result of this type of difficulty tends to be that people with AS do become rigid thinkers. Once they have devised a way of doing something, they will stick to it, and not be willing to try other ways. They will also tend to avoid trying anything new. This strategy helps them to reduce their anxiety, and avoid having to face the difficult tasks of remembering and doing something with a lot of new information each time they face any given problem. However, it also creates other problems for them, because if other things change, they find it very hard to adapt. If you are trying to help someone with AS change the way they do things, you need to keep this problem of rigidity in mind too.

Remembering to remember

What about those situations where the person with AS knows what he or she should be doing, but still forgets to do it? Often, the person fails to do some routine task, such as change their socks and underwear, despite many, many, reminders. If challenged, they can often tell you that they should do this every day, but still it does not happen. Carers can find this kind of forgetting very frustrating. It may feel as if the person is being deliberately stubborn.

It is unlikely, however, that this is deliberate stubbornness. In order to understand this problem, it is necessary to have some understanding of how another system in the brain works. The front parts of the brain (frontal areas, or frontal lobes) are very important to our social functioning. They are the part of the brain which is most affected in AS, and also in other relatively common conditions such as Alzheimer's disease, or mild brain injury (such as after a car accident).

These areas of the brain deal with attention, short-term memory, planning, organization, and sequencing of actions. If these areas of the brain do not work very well, then the person genuinely struggles to do what is asked of them. It is rather like having a physical disability and trying to be a marathon runner. However hard someone may try, they will not be able to run a marathon as well as someone who does not have that disability. No amount of criticism or punishment will make any difference to that.

In addition to dealing with attention and short-term memory, these frontal areas of the brain also control our ability to start an activity, and to stop doing it. When the frontal areas are severely damaged, the person may be unable to 'get going' on an activity or, once started, may be unable to stop. (The latter is known as 'perseveration'.) In cases of severe brain injury, people can become extremely passive, and just sit unless prompted into activity, or they get 'stuck' in an activity, doing the same thing over and over again, because they cannot stop.

In less severe cases, the person may have great trouble getting started on anything because they cannot organize themselves effectively, and this is the kind of difficulty usually seen in AS. The person may know what they should do, but may not be able to 'get themselves going' to actually do it. Consequently, even when the person with AS knows exactly what they should do, their difficulty is in getting themselves organized and making it happen.

So, after lots of repetition and reminders, a person with AS may learn that they should change their underwear and socks every day. As a result, their carers can say 'They know what they should be doing.' However, if their brain has to remember and get started on this activity without help, they may still not be able to do it. Even with prompting, the problems may still remain. This difficulty might be termed 'remembering to remember'.

We have already noted that people with AS are distractible (i.e. they have poor attention), so if anything else happens to distract them when they are starting out on an activity, they will still forget what they are doing. In order to remember something, it has to be the focus of attention for a while, and if the attention is distracted elsewhere, then the instruction or activity will be forgotten. In most people, we call this 'absent-mindedness' and it is not unusual, especially as people get older. People with AS have an extreme form of this.

> *Brian knows that he has a bad memory, and worries about it, as it often gets him into trouble. He has worked out a way to prevent himself forgetting what he is supposed to do. If someone asks him to do something, he repeats it over and over again to himself until he has completed the task.*

This works reasonably well unless he is interrupted, but it means that people think he is odd because he talks to himself.

People with AS are often described as odd, and often this arises from their very real social difficulties. However, sometimes, as with Brian, their oddities can be understood as attempts to cope with a complex and demanding world. Often they are aware that they are likely to fail in other people's eyes, and this adds to their general anxiety. As we all know, anxiety does not help one to remember, so one problem adds to another. If Brian realizes that he is likely to fail, he is more likely to worry about it next time round, and so probably more likely than ever to forget! No wonder he becomes anxious.

How does all this affect everyday life?

We have seen that people with AS have poor attention, which leads to them being distractible and forgetful. Information which is not properly attended to gets lost. They also have problems with understanding language, especially if this is complicated or sentences are long, and problem-solving, because lots of information is difficult to remember. In everyday life these difficulties cause a lot of problems:

- Knowing that one has a problem remembering things adds to the person's general anxiety. This in turn can make memory even worse.

- The person is seen as stubborn, rude or deliberately difficult, because they do not do what is asked of them.

- The person may forget really important things such as taking medicines, or paying their rent.

- The person may be so forgetful that they are unsafe. For example, they may leave the gas on, or fail to lock doors.

- They may forget important instructions or appointments.

- Personal hygiene may be poor because they forget to carry out routine tasks such as bathing, changing clothes, cleaning, etc.

- Their surroundings may become unhygienic because they cannot organize themselves sufficiently to clean, or throw away rubbish, or they forget to do so.

- The failure to remember can lead to anxious, repetitive questions, aimed at gaining reassurance. This can be very irritating to those around the person with AS, and may drive people away.

This is not, of course, an exhaustive list. Most people who know someone with AS could probably add to it. These problems will be more acute if the person with AS is trying to live on their own.

Can anything be done?

The first, and most important, thing to do is to try to get away from the idea that any of this behaviour is designed to 'wind you up'. It may indeed wind you up, but it is very unlikely that this is done deliberately. The problems arise from a fault in the way that the person's brain works. It may be quite a small fault, but the impact of it can be significant. The person with AS cannot help having this condition, and has no idea how he or she is making you feel.

The second thing to do is accept that the person *cannot* easily change. They are not going to be 'cured' of this problem.

However, there are various strategies that may help. While people with AS have problems of memory and language, their visual memory is usually good, and significantly better than their verbal memory. In other words, they will remember pictures better than words. This can be a useful channel for helping them to process and remember information. Wherever possible, when trying to communicate something that must be remembered, use pictures as well as, or instead of, words.

The strategies usually used to aid memory are not complicated, but they need planning, and the person with AS will usually need help to set them up. Most of these strategies are intended to supplement whatever memory skills the person has, and the aim is to promote as much independence as possible. This helps to lighten the load on those who are trying to care for the person with AS, and it also helps the person to feel more independent, which is good for their self-esteem. However, you will need to spend time explaining the new strategies to the person with AS, and getting them to accept that a new approach can be helpful. Remember that change can be seen as a threat, so you will need to be tactful and gentle in your approach.

Using plans and timetables

It may be that as someone who supports a person with AS, you have continued to hope that one day they will be able to remember to do things independently. You may have felt that they were being deliberately awkward, and that if only you could get through to them, things would change. Let yourself off the hook, and accept right now that this will not happen. The problems of AS are 'hard-wired'. That is, they are the result of brain differences that will not change. The person with AS is the way they are, and you will have to try to accept this, however difficult it may be. You cannot expect that the person with AS will make all the changes. You will have to change your own thinking and actions too. You need to accept that you will probably always have to remind the person of some things, or they will not happen. Once you can accept this, it may actually become less irritating. It can become part of what you do, as much as brushing your teeth every morning. If, however, you can get the person to use a timetable or plan, then in time you may be able to simply prompt them to check their plan for the day. This will be less tiresome than having to remind them of every activity throughout the day. To a large extent it will depend on the severity of their condition, and their overall level of ability.

> *Joe lives in a community home with three other young men who have AS. Their support workers have worked out a daily timetable for each of the four young men. These timetables include personal care activities such as bathing, cleaning teeth and washing hair, as well as domestic chores around the house, which they all share. In addition each young man's timetable allows some time for his particular work or educational commitments, interests, outings and visits.*
>
> *Every morning, when they get up, they each have a hot drink, and talk through what they are going to do that day. Each person's keyworker goes through the timetable (which is stuck on the wall in each of their bedrooms) with them, outlining the plan for the day, and any changes that might be necessary. Then the support workers encourage the young person to start with their personal care activities, and work from there.*

The levels of help or supervision that people with AS need can vary enormously. Some people with AS can be very independent, and rarely need help, except if something unusual happens, while others will need help and prompting to get through the simplest tasks. Aim to encourage as much independence as possible, without taking unnecessary risks.

For some people with AS it may be enough to have an ordinary calendar or diary readily available, so that they can write down things they need to remember. More able people can often be persuaded into the habit of writing lists and memos for themselves as aids to memory. Some will enjoy using a portable computer or 'Blackberry' type of technology. However, it is important that written notes all go in one place, such as a large desk diary, or lots of pieces of paper will soon get lost. This is where the liking of routines and rituals can be useful. You can work towards encouraging useful habits that will support their poor memory.

An individualized plan or timetable can save a lot of worry and uncertainty. It helps to encourage independence, and provide reassurance. There are many types of office planner available that can be adapted, and more recently planners for use at home with columns for each member of the family have started to appear. These could also be used in community homes with several residents. You can, of course, make your own.

Make a point of having the plan of the day, week or month (depending on the needs of the person with AS) up on the wall, in a place that will be easily and regularly seen. This might be in a bedroom, kitchen or by the front door. Colour code activities, so that similar things have the same colour. For less able people, large pictures indicating the activity may help. For more able people, a word or short phrase that indicates the activity will usually be enough.

A plan or timetable of any kind will often be enough to reduce, or even stop, the kind of anxious repetitive questioning which can be the result of not being able to remember what is going to happen. However, beware! For some people, it can actually make things worse, especially if the person has little sense of time. A planned visit, even when happily anticipated, can result in many questions of the kind 'Is it Tuesday yet?' You need to be flexible and see what works best for each individual.

> *Jeremy lives in a large home for people with learning disabilities. He has a mild learning disability, as well as his diagnosis of AS. Jeremy finds it very worrying when staffing changes mean that the people he expects to see when the shifts change are not there. As a consequence, he constantly asks the care staff in the home 'Who is on duty this afternoon/evening/tomorrow morning?' and this becomes very trying for the people who look after him.*
>
> *They have agreed a strategy amongst themselves that seems to help. If Jeremy asks about the staff rota, they all say the same thing: that he must check the staff rota which is displayed in the kitchen. If there is a change in staffing because of sickness or holidays, one member of staff will take Jeremy to one side and explain slowly and carefully who is not coming, and who will take their place. This has greatly reduced Jeremy's anxious questions.*

A timetable can also help with problems such as failing to remember to change underwear or bring down the dirty washing. If such activities are included on the timetable at regular times, and are colour coded too, then this can help greatly. Of course the person has to remember to consult the timetable every morning, but at least they only have to remember one thing, not several. Alternatively, if they need prompting, they only need to be prompted to do one thing, not each task of the day. They can also go back and look at the timetable as many times as they need to, so if they forget anything, they can go and check. This gives them reassurance and enables them to learn at their own pace. Eventually they may also begin to remember the timetable, even if they still need help to make the activities on it happen.

If written timetables or lists do not seem to help, then you may need to experiment. Making use of the visual strengths mentioned earlier can work better for some people.

> *One of Joe's housemates, Jim, has more problems than Joe and the others. He finds it difficult to cope with seeing his whole day's activities spread out before him. This makes him highly anxious. The carers have found that it works better if Jim's timetable is made up of a series of cards, each with one task on it, portrayed by a picture. The cards are in a holder, so that only the front one can be seen. When that task is finished, the front card is removed, so Jim can see the next card, and the next item on his timetable. He finds this approach more helpful, and less anxiety-provoking.*

The most difficult part of introducing a new system like this is to get the person or people with AS to accept it initially. The need to change will always feel threatening to someone with AS. For children, or younger people, it can help to present this as a rule of the house: 'Every morning we look at our timetable', as in Joe's house described above. People with AS tend to like rules. Rules are predictable, and make the world seem a safer place. Perhaps other members of the family or group could each have a timetable too, so that the person with AS does not feel the odd one out. Even if the other people do not use their timetables as regularly as the person with AS, it may help that such plans exist. Siblings will sometimes help with these in a home situation, and ease the burden of care for parents.

Building a routine

Because people with AS like rules, routines and rituals, it pays to use this to try and establish useful patterns of behaviour, such as self-care, house-cleaning, washing clothes and cooking meals. It may help to allocate set tasks to different days of the week. People with AS do not find this restrictive as many people might. Routine and sameness make them feel safe. The use of a written or pictorial timetable can be very helpful in establishing these kinds of routines. This is usually easier to do with younger people who have not already got too set into their own routines.

David is a teenager, who lives with his parents and his older sister at home. He is an able youngster in many ways, but finds it difficult to remember to do ordinary everyday things such as bathing and changing his clothes. David's sister is very fond of him, and makes a point of going to his room every morning to help him choose what to wear each day. She also reminds him that he needs to have a shower before he gets dressed. David accepts his sister's help without a problem, but if his mother tries to do the same, he gets upset and angry, saying 'I don't need my mum to tell me what to do. I'm not a baby!'

David's sister is going to go to university. The family are worried what will happen when she leaves. Before the day of her departure arrives, she spends a lot of time explaining to David what will happen when she goes, and letting him know that she will still phone and visit him regularly. She also draws up a timetable for David which together they stick on his bedroom wall. She gradually helps him to get used to looking at the timetable, rather than waiting for her to come and help him. Thus, when she finally leaves, David is prepared, and less distressed. He also feels pleased that he can be more independent too.

It may be harder to introduce this approach to someone who is older, because they will have become more set in their ways. However, if someone is already aware that they are struggling and want help, they may be more open to new ideas. Many will welcome this approach, as David in the above example, because it enables them to be more independent. Much will depend on whether or not the person with AS perceives that there is a problem. It may take some tactful discussion at first, to get them to acknowledge an area of difficulty.

If at first the person with AS is reluctant to use a plan or timetable, you will need to sit down with them and explain in detail how the idea will work, and why you think it will help them. You may have to go over this several times. You might even suggest a small reward if they agree to try it out. However, be careful not to make this sound childish or patronizing. Sometimes a word of praise might be enough, or perhaps arranging a favourite treat or outing will help. You will have to judge what seems most appropriate for the person you are supporting. It is important not to sound patronizing or insulting, while still being realistic about the person's problems. Most importantly of all, be encouraging.

One strategy that can work is to promise to spend some time with the person, discussing their favourite topic or interest, *after* they have completed certain necessary tasks. As you probably know, talking about this interest is something they will always be keen to do. In reality, you will probably do all the listening and they will talk, and it will probably be rather boring for you! However, if you decide to try this, it is important that you keep your side of the bargain, or it will not work. People with AS often like company, and want to spend some time with others, but it is very much on their terms. This tends to drive many people away, so it is likely that to promise (and give) them some time and attention doing what they most enjoy will be a valuable reward.

Other kinds of encouragement might be the promise of an outing or other favourite activity, once the routine tasks are completed. However, you may need to be inventive and experiment with things that you think will be rewarding. You could also ask the person to suggest things for themselves. However you decide to proceed, you will need to have their co-operation in the process. Remember that any change is likely to feel threatening. Sometimes the payoff for changing will simply be to reduce the difficulties which they have previously experienced. If someone has been struggling for some time, they may be grateful for any suggestions to improve their situation. However, do not forget that people with AS find change particularly difficult and anxiety-provoking, so do not expect rapid changes.

Aiding understanding

As we have seen, the problems with attention and memory affect how people with AS can process language. Long sentences are difficult to remember, and the person may have trouble responding appropriately, simply because there is too much information given to hold on to.

The key to using language with somebody who has AS is to keep sentences short and simple. Never include more than one idea or instruction. Make sure that the person has processed and understood what you are saying before you move on to something else. People can sometimes get very good at appearing to understand, by nodding and smiling, when they have no idea at all of what you are saying. Ask questions to make sure that they have heard and really understood. This is particularly important if they are already doing something else, however small, when you ask them.

Aiding problem-solving

Both the attention and memory problems typical of AS also contribute to difficulties of problem-solving. In order to solve a problem, you have to understand exactly what the problem is, and be able to think about possible solutions. To choose between these solutions, you have to be able to hold them in your memory at the same time and compare them. For people with AS, this process is very difficult. To help and support someone with AS, it is important to think creatively about how to ease this process, perhaps using some of the ideas suggested above, such as making notes or drawings, or using other forms of reminders. However, it is also important to think about the way you communicate with the person, focusing particularly on keeping your messages short and simple, or there is a risk that you confuse rather than help.

Unwanted help

What if the person with AS resents being given help and wants to manage alone, even though they clearly have problems of memory and attention? This is not uncommon, and can pose severe problems. It seems to be particularly common when the person who has AS has not received a diagnosis early in life. They may have some awareness that they have problems, but do not understand why, and resent the fact that they feel different. This may lead to an angry rejection of attempts to help, even from close family or friends.

Mike lives alone in a house that used to belong to his parents. He used to live with them when they were alive, and his mother always gave him a lot of help. However, both his father and mother have now died, and Mike remains alone in the family house. His only sister is married and lives a few miles away. She tries to help Mike but he resents what he considers her interference, and he gets very angry with her.

Mike's sister approaches the authorities for help for Mike, as she is worried what will happen to him when she can no longer help. She is worried that he is very forgetful, and often leaves doors unlocked and the gas cooker turned on all night. On one occasion he flooded the bathroom because he forgot that he had left the bath taps on. He also forgets to put his rubbish out for collection, so that the house gets filled with bags of rubbish, which smell and are unhygienic. Mike's sister believes that he has Asperger syndrome, based on what she has read, but he has never received a formal diagnosis and she does not believe that he would co-operate in a diagnostic process.

She is distressed to be told that unless Mike agrees to have help, nobody can insist that he does so. Outside authorities can only intervene if he becomes a serious danger to himself or others. Mike has argued with his neighbours, and threatened one of them in the past, but he has never actually done anything seriously dangerous. Unless something more serious occurs, the law does not allow others to interfere with Mike's independent life, even when he is clearly not coping very well.

As a parent, family member or carer, you may have to accept that you cannot make someone accept help if they do not want it. All you can do is keep a watching eye, and make it clear that you will be available to help if you can. Sometimes you just have to let someone fail before they will acknowledge that they need help. Even then, sometimes people will struggle on alone, living on the edge of safety. Unless they are a serious risk to themselves or others, there is little that you can do.

SUMMARY

o People with AS suffer from problems of attention and concentration, which in turn affect memory, especially short-term memory. They can, however, have a very good long-term memory, often remembering information that is of interest to them in great detail. This tends to lead to misunderstandings with those who care for them, who find it hard to believe there is a problem with memory when such detail can be recalled.

o Short-term memory requires the person to pay attention and register the information given. If they cannot do this effectively, then the information does not remain in memory. People with AS find it harder to pay attention, and to maintain that attention for any length of time, so they have trouble remembering what is said to them, or things that happened recently. This is the result of poor functioning of the frontal parts of the brain. When they are helped to pay attention, or do so because of particular interest, and as a result repeat things many times, they can remember, often in great detail.

o People with AS often have trouble recalling learned information when it is needed in a particular moment or situation. They may need prompting to remember what has to be done, even when they know it well if asked. This problem also has its roots in the frontal areas of the brain, and might be termed 'remembering to remember'. This means that they may know what should be done, but still forget to do it, unless reminded.

o   Timetables, plans and routines can all help with these problems, as can sympathetic and patient helpers, whether these are family, friends or paid carers. However, these helpers need to learn how to help, by using strategies for giving regular reminders, and by keeping language simple and instructions short. They also need to be able to accept that the person with AS cannot easily change, and many of these problems will always be there.

o   Frustratingly, if the person with AS does not want to accept help, then little can be done unless they are a serious risk to themselves or others.

Chapter 4

Practical Difficulties and Everyday Tasks

We have already noted that many people with Asperger syndrome are bright, some much brighter than the average. Despite this, they may have difficulties with everyday living which can be unexpected. If the person appears able, other people tend to assume that they will be able to cope with normal everyday activities without any problem. Unfortunately this is not always the case. Many areas of everyday life can pose challenges to those with AS, and, for those who have not been diagnosed early in life, the failure to recognize and understand their difficulties may have added to their problems.

Where a person has grown into an adult without anyone understanding the real cause of their difficulties, then those around them will not have been able to provide the kind of detailed teaching and support that can make the difference between a relatively well-ordered life and one which deteriorates into disorder. If children with AS are helped to develop good routines of personal care and hygiene early in life, this can stand them in good stead later on, even if they still need some reminders. If, however, the AS has not been recognized, then the child will often grow into an adult who is unable to cope with personal care, or keeping their surroundings in order, and who generally finds coping with life very difficult.

Jon lived alone after his elderly mum died. He was fiercely independent and resented anyone trying to help him. He had only barely tolerated his mother's efforts to keep the home clean and tidy. She had ensured that he bathed and changed his clothes at least once a week, but even that had been a battle. After she died, Jon's personal care deteriorated. His room was full of piles of dirty clothes, and both he and the house smelt. Jon never cooked properly. He bought ready-made meals and cooked them in the microwave. The sink was soon full of dirty dishes growing mould.

Yet Jon was an intelligent man. He had a passionate interest in astronomy, and loved reading books about it. He also had a collection of DVDs on various aspects of astronomy, and would spend hours watching these. He could talk for hours about the solar system, and how it had developed. So how could it be that he completely failed to carry out these basic self-care and domestic activities? On the face of it, this seems quite irrational, but this kind of mismatch is not uncommon in those with AS.

In the last chapter, we saw that because of the way their brains are different, people with Asperger syndrome have difficulty in maintaining their attention. This leads to problems of memory, unless they make considerable efforts to remember. Even then, they may have trouble remembering the information they need at the right time, without help. We have noted also that these differences in brain function mean that people with AS may have great difficulty in planning and organizing their activities. When faced with a task which is made up of several steps, they are often unable to see where to start. The related difficulties in sequencing and making use of feedback will also have a significant effect on the way that people with AS can cope with everyday life.

Difficulties with sequencing mean that people with AS may forget one part of an activity, get things in the wrong order, or simply lose where they have got to. This is likely to make it difficult for them to complete complex tasks without help. It also adds to the difficulty of organizing themselves when faced with a range of tasks.

The difficulties in processing feedback mean that people with AS may have trouble learning from their experiences. Either they fail to notice that they have got things wrong or, if they do notice, they fail to make the connection between what they have done and the outcome. This area of difficulty contributes significantly to the social problems that many people with AS experience, because they fail to see how their behaviour affects others.

Self-care and personal hygiene

The person with AS may frequently neglect personal hygiene by, for example:

- forgetting basic regular self-care such as washing, hair-washing, cleaning teeth, etc.

- forgetting to change or wash clothes regularly

- forgetting to attend dental or doctor's appointments.

The main difficulty with these kinds of activities is not usually a lack of skills. The person concerned is usually quite capable of carrying out the various tasks, but they simply do not think about doing so. Sometimes they might start out intending to have a shower, for example, but become distracted by something they see, and wander off to do something completely different. Alternatively, they may simply not know where to begin. When a task requires several stages for completion, they may forget a stage, forget where they are in the sequence, or just not know how to get started. A failure to keep themselves clean and tidy can add to their social difficulties too, by putting other people off.

> *Bob was a young man with Asperger syndrome, who was desperate to find a girlfriend. He knew what his ideal woman would look like, and was always on the lookout for her. One day, while attending his computer class at college, he saw someone who looked like his ideal. However, when he approached her to try to talk to her, she just looked him up and down and turned away. Bob was very hurt and puzzled. What he did not realize was that his hair was greasy and untidy, his clothes were grubby, and he smelt rather strongly because he rarely bathed. Bob did not understand that in failing to present himself well, he stood little chance of succeeding in his quest.*

Establishing good routines, and setting up a timetable for personal care and laundry, can help with these problems. Ideally, many of those who live alone would benefit from someone visiting regularly, who could build a good, supportive relationship, and who would remind the person with AS to follow their timetables and routines.

For those who are very forgetful, timetables and calendars need to be large, colourful and placed where they will not be missed. Different coloured pens, or markers, for different kinds of activities can help to distinguish between them. Most people with AS will need help to set this up, and care needs to be taken that the system doesn't appear childish or insulting to an adult. Office wall planners can be a good way of setting up this kind of timetable, as they have an appropriately adult and businesslike feel.

Where someone lives in a shared house, it may be possible to set up regular routines for bathing, cleaning, cooking and shopping which apply to everyone. This avoids singling out the person with AS and making them feel they are the odd one out.

Clothing

The following behaviours may cause difficulties:

- wearing the wrong clothes for the weather, or wearing odd clothes

- insisting on always wearing the same colour, or the same clothes

- disliking new clothes, or particular items of clothing.

Wearing the wrong clothes can occur because the person with AS either has little awareness of what is expected or does not notice or care what others think. They may choose unusual combinations of style or colours, and be unaware that other people may find these strange. Sometimes their odd choices may be because they have little sensitivity to cold or heat, so they may wear shorts in winter, or woollen jumpers in a heatwave.

An attachment to particular items of clothing, or a particular colour, often has its roots in the person's dislike of change. The person with AS likes things to stay the same, and wearing the same old clothes over and over again is comforting and reassuring. Clean clothes may feel stiff and uncomfortable. They may also resist buying or wearing new clothes because they are not so comfortable. Some items of clothing may be rejected because they are just not comfortable, either in design or fabric. Labels in the back of items like T-shirts or jumpers can be extremely irritating to some people.

Useful strategies here might include setting up regular routines for changing and washing clothes, and making sure that the washing powders or liquids used are not too strongly smelling. The acceptance of new clothes may be helped by making sure that they are always washed with the existing laundry before they are worn. This will make them softer, and also make them smell the same as the existing clothes. It may also be helpful to try to help the person to buy new clothes which are as similar as possible to their old ones in style and colour, and which are made of natural fabrics, or soft ones such as fleece. Labels which irritate can be cut out. As this problem is often associated with having sensitive skin, all these strategies can help to avoid discomfort. Some people with AS, like many people with autism, can be particularly sensitive to textures.

Where the problem is that the choice of clothes is eccentric, or the person always prefers the same colour, this will need to be handled more tactfully. Everyone is entitled to their personal choices, and really it does not matter if they choose to wear unusual clothes, unless their outfit makes them stand out so much that they become a target for bullying or ridicule. In this case, it may be possible to gently suggest more acceptable alternatives. For example, a baseball cap is probably less likely to give rise to comment that a knitted bobble hat!

Fred tended to raise a smile wherever he went. He lived alone, and always shopped at the local shops, where he was well known. He enjoyed greeting all the local shopkeepers as his friends, and doing his modest weekly shop was part of his social diary. However, wearing his cycle shorts, red parka jacket and striped, knitted woolly hat, he did not realize that he was a figure of fun. One day, a gang of teenagers started to shout and jeer at him, because of his odd appearance. Fred was frightened and ran home. He is now worried about going shopping on his own again.

This kind of experience can make someone with AS fearful of going out, but sometimes an unpleasant episode like this may make the person more amenable to considering a change. However, this is a difficult area, and will need to be tackled with great tact.

Hygiene and cleanliness at home

The following problems frequently occur for people with AS:

- not being able to keep their room, kitchen or house clean and tidy

- forgetting to put out rubbish or collect milk, post, etc.

- leaving food in the cupboard or fridge until it is out of date or mouldy

- not maintaining their house or garden.

Keeping things clean and tidy is again a matter of personal choice, to some extent. However, when the person's surroundings become so chaotic that they keep losing things, or they are actually unhygienic, then action may need to be taken. In many cases, the person with AS will themselves find the chaos frustrating, but simply not know how to put it right. As with the personal care issues, the failure to keep their surroundings clean and hygienic is often the result of forgetting, and being unable to plan, rather than a lack of skills.

Many household tasks have several stages, and thus the person with AS may find it difficult to know where to begin, or how to organize the task. Very often it will be a case of 'out of sight, out of mind' and they will simply not think about a job which needs doing because it is not visible. The person with AS is unlikely to be motivated by worries about what other people might think, because they will not be able to 'put themselves into someone else's shoes' and see things from there. However, they can get frustrated by their own inability to keep their surroundings as they would like them to be.

Len lives alone, and prefers to do so. He likes having his own place, and being able to keep it as he likes. Unfortunately, he is not very good at tidying and cleaning, so it is not long before the place is full of rubbish, and Len cannot find what he wants. He gets very frustrated with himself, and on one occasion smashed a load of dishes which had piled up in the sink. He could not cope with organizing the large amount of washing up that was waiting to be done. Since then, Len's sister comes to see him once a week, and together they tidy and clean the flat until it is back to how Len likes it. This seems to be a good compromise. Len trusts his sister, and she can check that everything is safe and in order on her weekly visit.

This kind of intermittent support may be all that is needed for some people. However, it does need to be handled carefully. It will be important that the person who comes to help is someone who is trusted. There is also the risk that the help will be seen as interference by the person with AS. However, with careful planning it can be a useful way of providing support to someone who is largely independent.

For others who need more support, a visual timetable as suggested for personal care, which is pinned on the wall where it will be seen every day, can be enormously helpful. Complicated tasks may need to be broken down into sections, and perhaps numbered, so that the correct sequence is obvious. It will be important, however, to make sure that this timetable is large and detailed, so that it is not easily overlooked. Even then, some people with AS will still need additional reminders to check it regularly.

For those who choose to live alone, a daily phone call reminder to look at their timetable may be all that is needed, if they are willing to co-operate. As with all of us, some people with AS are more amenable than others. If the person does not feel that their way of life is a problem, there may be little that can be done to help, unless the situation becomes critical.

Food, cooking and shopping

The following kinds of difficulties are not uncommon for people with AS:

- being unable to plan a meal or buy ingredients for a meal without help

- not being able to cook a meal independently

- living off pre-prepared foods

- having very fixed ideas about what they will and won't eat

- having rigid routines around food, such as fish always on a Friday, and being very resistant to change.

Some of these difficulties arise for the same reason as those with personal care and cleaning. The person may forget what has to be done, forget how to do it, or simply not know where to begin with the task. With help to plan and organize the task, they may have the necessary skills to cook a good meal, but will need prompting and reminding through the various stages. Getting the various steps in the right order can be difficult for some people with AS, and here again a numbered sequence of things to do can help. Failing that, a caring person to help and oversee will enable the person with AS to feel a sense of achievement when they can produce a home-cooked meal.

Rosie loves cooking. She feels very proud when she can cook a meal for members of her family, or a group of friends. However, she finds it very hard to follow a recipe without help. Rosie and her mother plan their meals, and do the shopping together. When it is Rosie's turn to cook, her mother is always at hand to help her with the recipe, and remind her where she has got to. Rosie has all the practical skills she needs to cook a meal, but without her mother's help in directing what she is doing, she soon gets lost and muddled.

Very often, if such help is not available, the person with AS will take the easier option, and buy pre-prepared meals to heat in a microwave. This is quite a reasonable strategy, but it may mean that the person does not eat a very healthy or balanced diet, especially if they tend to eat the same meals regularly. As with many other aspects of life, people with AS dislike change, so they will often tend to eat the same things over and over again. In part, this may be because they find it difficult to think of alternatives. In extreme cases, however, they may only accept foods of one type, or colour. People with AS may also have particular sensitivities, disliking certain flavours or textures.

Once established, unusual eating patterns like this can be hard to change. This is not specific to people with AS. Many people who do not have AS are happy to take the easy option, and buy ready-cooked meals, and will tend to stick with what is familiar. There is a fine line between what is personal choice and when unusual eating patterns become a real problem. The main concern is that the person with AS eats a reasonably healthy, balanced diet, or health problems will undoubtedly follow.

One approach to improve someone's diet might be to look at the range of pre-prepared meals available in the local shops, and work out a weekly plan which will provide a more balanced diet. At least part of the difficulty for many people with AS is the process of making a choice. Making the choices with them, in advance, can be enormously helpful. If someone can help them to plan a weekly menu, and this is written down and kept somewhere visible, then they are more likely to be able to stick to it.

You will probably also need to explain several times why it is important to eat a range of different foods for good health. It is also important to give a careful explanation as to why food should not be kept too long, and this will probably have to be repeated many times too. If you can provide a simple rule, such as 'the fridge must be emptied once a week, and everything that is out of date thrown away', that may help. We have already noted that people with AS usually like rules, because they make life predictable and easier to manage. This approach will not work, however, if you simply try to impose your own views on the person with AS, without proper discussion. As with anyone, they will probably resent this, and keep to their own way of doing things.

It is also important to remember that it will never be enough to explain once. Remember that the person with AS has problems of attention, concentration and short-term memory. They may fail to register what you have said, recall only part of it, or forget it completely, because they happen to have been distracted at the critical moment. They are not being deliberately difficult. Think about someone telling you a long phone number that you want to remember when you are in the middle of a busy party. Unless you write it down immediately, it is very unlikely that you will remember it.

For much of the time, life is like this for those with Asperger syndrome. You will need to write things down, go over them several times and probably still have to remind the person from time to time.

Another strategy that may help them improve their overall diet is to help them to cook a proper meal at least once or twice a week. Alternatively, there may be one or more friends or family members who will be willing to cook a meal for the person regularly, or even occasionally. This can give the person with AS a variety of social contacts as well as a better diet, and will avoid all the responsibility falling on a single person. However, you do need to be flexible too. Even if their choice of diet is unconventional, if it is basically healthy and includes a range of foods, then it may be better simply to accept that this is the way they choose to eat.

Like cooking, shopping for a meal is quite a complex activity, and shopping for a whole week even more so. Someone with AS may be quite overwhelmed by the complexity of such a task, and so refuse even to try, unless they have help. Furthermore, dealing with money to pay for shopping may pose an additional challenge for some people. This problem can be helped by forward planning of favourite meals, with a shopping list associated with each one. Similarly there can be a shopping list allied to keeping clothes and the home clean, so that washing powder and cleaning materials are always available. However, because these are complicated tasks, it will probably be necessary for someone else to help with any shopping that is more complicated than shopping for a single meal.

For those who are computer literate, it may be possible to teach them to shop online. This has the advantage that the supermarket websites keep a record of what you buy each week, and you can simply re-order what you have bought before, on a regular basis. This will have to be handled carefully though, because payment will usually have to be made by credit card, and managing the card may itself cause problems. Furthermore, if one item is not used regularly and stocks build up, the person with AS may not think to cancel that item and could end up with dozens! Another issue with supermarket shopping is that the food is delivered all at once, and will need to be sorted and put away. For someone with AS this may be too difficult a task to manage alone.

Handling money and paying bills

The following kinds of problems often occur:

- losing important letters or documents and failing to pay bills

- being unable to plan a budget and keep to it

- being exploited by others.

Handling money, budgeting and paying bills are all complex activities which require a number of stages, and are much more difficult than simply adding up numbers. Many people with AS can add up, and know the value of money, but find that managing their finances is beyond them. Some people with AS simply forget to pay bills, and get into trouble in consequence.

Sometimes people with AS fail to appreciate the importance of paying the regular, and perhaps boring, bills for electricity, water, gas and so on. They would much rather spend their money on food treats, music, books or videos, and cannot understand that these might be much less important than the former. This can be a particular problem for those who are less able. Others are just overwhelmed by the complexity of dealing with bills and money, and will either ignore the bills, hide them, or throw them away.

Ben was very pleased when he moved into his own flat. He was very happy that at last he could be independent. However, it was not long before problems began to develop. Ben could not organize himself to clean his flat, and it soon became very untidy, and very dirty. In addition, he kept losing things. He lost the electricity bill, and as a result it was not paid. He did not realize there was a problem until the electricity was cut off.

If the person with AS has a carer or family member they trust, it may be possible for this person to manage these difficulties by helping them to develop a system of paying bills regularly, perhaps by direct debit, and to draw up a budget. However, they will almost certainly need help to stick to this. It will be no good setting it up and leaving them to it. Handling money can be a real problem for some people with AS, especially when it comes to setting budgets and keeping to them. If the person is living alone, it may be helpful to assist them in setting up several bank or saving accounts, so that there is, for example, one for spending money, one for food, one for emergencies and one for holidays. This can help to avoid overspending and make the process of managing money much clearer. Paying important bills by direct debit or standing order can also be very helpful.

Another difficulty that may arise in managing money is that the person with AS is vulnerable to exploitation. This can happen for two reasons. Either the person has a limited understanding of money, and is easily persuaded to part with it, or they spend their money on others in an attempt to buy friendship.

Ernie was a good looking young man, who had no trouble finding girlfriends. They would persuade him to take them to expensive restaurants and buy them clothes. Because he was so easy-going and eager to please them, he always did as they asked. However, because he behaved oddly, and did not join in with their friends, they would soon tire of him and move on. Ernie was always in debt, as he moved from one girlfriend to another. He became known as an 'easy touch' and all the local girls took a turn at separating Ernie from his money. He could never understand why these relationships ended, and was always hopeful that if he spent enough on the next girl, she would stay.

If the person with AS struggles with managing their money, but resents outside interference, it may be worth seeking legal advice, to see what options there are. Some people with AS are very reluctant to spend their money, and become highly suspicious of anyone trying to help. They may make unfounded accusations, so you need to ensure that you, as well as they, are protected.

Timekeeping

People with AS often have different sleep patterns from the majority of people. They may be awake late into the night, and sleep in the day. They also have difficulty in organizing their time, and keeping to a timetable, without help. Common problems include:

- being unable to get to appointments on time without help
- forgetting important appointments
- failing to get up in time to get to work
- sleeping all day and staying up all night.

These difficulties can cause particular problems when the person with AS shares their living space with others, and can often get them into trouble with partners, parents, neighbours and bosses. At times, the person themselves will get very angry and upset because they have missed an activity or event that they wished to attend. Clearly, in these kind of situations, the person with AS needs help to plan and keep to a timetable.

We have already noted in the last chapter that the problems of attention and short-term memory, which trouble most people with AS, can result in their forgetting important appointments and dates. Once again, careful management of a timetable or diary can be enormously helpful. However, it is unlikely that most people with AS will be able to manage this without some help. If the person is someone who is interested in technology, they may appreciate having a mobile phone, or portable computer, which gives them visual or audible warnings of appointments. These often have alarms which can be set up on a daily, weekly, monthly or even yearly basis, as well as reminders for specific events. Even so, some people with AS will need help to learn how to use these items, and will probably need help to program in their particular appointments.

Problems with the sleeping and waking cycle are more difficult to manage, because these do appear to be part of the condition of AS. Changing an established sleep pattern can be difficult. It is not advisable to use medication to help sleep, except for very short periods, as this can often be addictive, and may produce other problems when the person stops taking it. For example, some sleeping tablets can produce nightmares on withdrawal.

People with AS often actively prefer the night-time, because it is dark and quiet. If they are a person who dislikes too much stimulation, the night-time can seem like a haven from the demands of daytime and other people. If the person with AS is a confirmed night-owl, but wants a job too, one approach might be to help them look for jobs which involve night shift work, as long as this is within their intellectual abilities. However, in this case it may be important to look for work which enables them to enjoy the quiet and darkness, rather than one which involves brightly lit factories and lots of other workers. A job as a night-watchman may be ideal, but you need to be sure that they understand the risks of such a job.

Alternatively, you may find that you can shift their sleeping pattern closer to a more normal one, by the regular use of a good alarm clock. If the person lives in a shared home, or a supported living setting, it may be possible to have someone wake them at the necessary time, and start them off on their early-morning routine, to get them off to work, school or college. This can make them tired enough to ensure that the person is then ready to sleep at a more conventional time in the evening. To some extent, establishing a good sleep routine is a matter of habit, and with persistence and support it may be possible to do this over a couple of weeks.

Keeping safe

We have seen that people with AS tend to be very forgetful and absent-minded, which can cause them a number of different problems. One of the most worrying is that these difficulties can result in them putting themselves or others at risk by, for example:

- failing to lock doors or close windows when they need to
- leaving the gas or electricity on unattended
- forgetting to turn off a tap
- not thinking to ask for help in the event of a leak or other emergency.

If someone is repeatedly forgetting things which could result in a dangerous situation, then every effort should be made to persuade them to accept some help and supervision in these areas. Simple practical adaptations can also help, such as installing taps that turn off automatically when you stop using them, and having an electric rather than a gas cooker. Sometimes a checklist of 'things to do before you leave the house' might help, but it will have to be in a prominent place or the person will forget to look at it!

> *Diane shared a flat with her friend from school, Sharon. Diane has Asperger syndrome. Sharon has always known that, and has helped Diane with lots of things throughout their schooldays. They decided to share a flat, and Diane's mother was very relieved, because Sharon would be able to keep an eye on Diane, and make sure she didn't get into difficulty. One weekend, Sharon went away to stay with her new boyfriend. Diane decided that she would cook some chips for herself. She turned on the cooker and put the pan of oil on to heat. Then she went upstairs to get changed. She forgot that she had put the pan on the cooker top, and decided to have a bath. She was enjoying a good soak when she smelt smoke. When she went downstairs she saw flames shooting out of the pan, and licking up the kitchen wall. Diane panicked and ran out of the flat in her dressing gown. She did not know what to do. Fortunately, a neighbour saw the flames and smoke and called the fire brigade.*

The difficulty here was that the situation changed. Sharon was no longer available to supervise, and Diane was her usual forgetful self. Although she knew the dangers of leaving a chip-pan unattended, she simply forgot about it, and began to do something else. This is not, of course, unique to those with AS. Many people, especially the elderly, can be equally absent-minded. However, this kind of forgetfulness can be dangerous. Both Diane and her neighbours were put at risk by her poor memory.

The effect on others

It is probably clear by now that these difficulties in coping with everyday living can put a huge strain on the relationships that the person with AS may have with others. If someone is dirty, untidy and unhygienic, this will not endear them to anyone who has to share their living space. If they fail to look after their surroundings and are noisy and careless too, then friends and neighbours may soon lose patience. Persistent lateness, or failing to turn up, will soon irritate the most kindly boss.

Sadly, the person with AS may be completely unaware that these problems are contributing to their difficulties in getting on with those around them. Often they feel angry and resentful that they cannot just get on with their life as they wish. Some people with AS are troubled by the fact that they cannot cope with these everyday matters, and are very grateful for any help or support they may get. Unfortunately, many people with AS do not see themselves as the root of the problem, and may resist all attempts to help. This can be very frustrating, and may even mean that they are putting others at risk, as with Diane above.

Some of these difficulties will put the person with AS at risk too. Bad food or an inadequate diet can soon make them ill, and failure to maintain and repair the home could make it dangerous. Failing to pay bills can result in, at worst, eviction or, at best, that services are cut off. Poor budgeting can lead to all kinds of difficulties. Wearing the wrong clothes may lead to catching cold, or simply being a target of fun, or even hostility, because the person looks odd. Thus, without adequate support, the everyday life of a person with AS can soon become exceedingly difficult.

Sources of support

It is not uncommon to find middle-aged adults with AS still living with ageing or elderly parents, who have provided support for years to ensure that they stay clean, live in hygienic surroundings and eat reasonable meals. If these parents come to a point where they can no longer offer support because of ill health or infirmity, or if they die, then it is not uncommon for a situation such as that described at the beginning of this chapter, with Jon, to develop.

Some people will be fortunate enough to have other sources of support, such as siblings, partners, friends or paid carers. Sometimes these kinds of support will be informal and infrequent, but will be enough to keep the person with AS safe and well. To a large extent, this will depend on that person's level of ability and learned skills, but their need for support is likely also to depend on the severity of their difficulties. People with AS can be very different, and in some cases their level of disability is very mild. Others will be much more affected, and will find it hard to live any kind of independent life, especially if the AS is associated with a mild learning disability.

If you are trying to support a person with AS, or someone you believe may have the condition, you may find that you have to be very careful and tactful in offering your help. Like most of us, the majority of people with AS do not like to be told what to do. Some will resent the implication that they have any kind of disability or problem, while others will be hugely grateful that someone realizes the nature of their difficulties. You will find that you will achieve a great deal more success with your attempts to help if you can avoid being critical, and try to maintain a positive and helpful attitude in suggesting new approaches. Of course, this is not always easy to do!

SUMMARY

o   People with Asperger syndrome often have trouble with a range of everyday tasks. This can be true even when they are very able intellectually.

o   The difficulties that they have are related to the particular differences in brain function that are typical of people with AS.

o   Personal care can be a problem, and this affects people's success in relationships and work.

o   Cooking, shopping and cleaning can all present difficulties because of the problems of organization and sequencing which are common to those with AS.

o   Managing money can be a problem, and people with AS often need help with budgeting.

o   People with AS may need help to keep themselves safe from exploitation.

o   Some people with AS resent the interference of others and may resist help. However, you cannot force them to accept help unless they are putting themselves or others at risk.

Chapter 5

Language and Conversation

Unlike children with autism, children with AS do not usually have an obvious language delay. They usually begin to speak at around one to two years old, and they acquire language at the normal rate. However, some parents do note that the child's first word can be unusual, so that instead of 'mummy' or 'daddy' their first word is something like 'aeroplane', or 'car'. Interestingly these first words usually refer to something inanimate, not a person or animal. Occasionally the child will be slow to speak, but once they start they can speak relatively well, and it is clear that they have been absorbing language for some time, even though not using it.

Often the oddities of the child's language are not really noticed until they mix with other children at school. If the child is the first or only child in a family, and the parents are not experienced with young children, they may not realize that their child is unusual in any way, until he or she starts to mix with others. Even where there are other children in the family, they may have become used to making allowances for the 'odd' child, and it will not be until others outside the family are encountered that the difficulties become really apparent. Some children with AS also have their own words for things, which can make them harder to understand when they are young. Sometimes these individual words may persist into adulthood.

However, the most obviously unusual aspect of their language is the way they speak. Children with AS used to sometimes be referred to as 'little professors' because they can talk at length about their special interest topic, sounding unusually grown-up and formal. This formal sounding language and use of long words usually persists into adulthood and, when added to their tendency to include a great deal of extra information in any reply they make, can make their conversation sound very odd. For example, one client of mine, when asked how his journey to see me had been, replied: 'Fine, thank you. The train arrived three minutes late, and the journey took twelve minutes. It took me another fifteen and a half minutes to walk from the station.'

This is typical of the kind of detailed reply one may get from someone with AS, and although it is quite correct it sounds odd. Added to this, people with AS often have difficulty regulating the sound of their voice, and frequently speak rather loudly, which adds to the apparent oddness of their communication. They may stress the wrong word in a sentence, sometimes inadvertently lending a different meaning from the one that they intended. At times they can also sound quite abrupt, and this can be misinterpreted as aggression.

Taking things literally

One of the odder features of language in those with AS is their tendency to take things literally. When they are children, this can often lead to comical misunderstandings, but also sometimes to real fears and even nightmares. Adults with AS can also be confused by these odd figures of speech. Imagine for a moment what you might think if you took the following statements literally:

- That curry blew my head off!
- I caught her eye.
- Pull your socks up.
- She's got eyes in the back of her head.
- I'll kill you if you do that!
- She needs a kick up the backside.
- Give me your hand.
- You make me sick!
- My head feels as if it is about to explode!
- He looks down at heel.
- She'll have your guts for garters!

Unfortunately, English is full of these quaint and colloquial expressions, and they can cause real confusion to people with AS, especially when they are young. However, even older people can remain confused by them, especially if they have never plucked up courage to ask anyone what they really meant. If the person with AS does not understand, it can lead to them being unnecessarily frightened of someone, or fearful that something bad will happen, when what was said was intended as a joke, or at worst a mild reprimand. Try to avoid using these kinds of expressions around people with AS. If, however, you forget and do use one, try to take a few minutes to make sure that they understand what you really mean. This can save a lot of confusion later.

Sometimes people with AS can take things literally in another way. If told on one occasion that they should not do something, they do not automatically generalize that to other, similar situations. They think that the reprimand applied to that one occasion only, and do not see that it might apply to others. For example, in a fit of temper, they might kick the door. On being told they should not kick the door, they may agree, but later be found kicking a different door in a temper. This is a *different* door, so the same rule does not apply in the person's mind. If you want to stop them from kicking any doors, you will have to be very explicit about it. 'You should not kick the door,' needs to become, 'You should never kick doors.' You may need to check that they understand that this rule applies to all doors, not just the current one.

Another area of difficulty may be when the intonation or stress given to a particular word can change the meaning of the sentence or phrase used. The person with AS may not process this difference, and could be confused by it. Consider these differences:

> *That* is my book – that object there is my book.

> That *is* my book – that is my book, not someone else's.

> That is *my* book – that is my book, not yours.

> That is my *book* – that is my book rather than anything else of mine.

These are quite subtle differences. However, they can be a real source of misunderstanding for someone with AS. If they seem not to have understood what you have said, consider whether this kind of difficulty may be at the root of the problem.

Difficulties with conversations

People with AS can easily lose track of a conversation, because of their poor attention. This can be frustrating both for the person with AS and the person who is trying to communicate with them. We have already noted that when someone is talking to them, it is often hard for the person with AS to hold on to all the information in a long sentence. If the surroundings are noisy or distracting in other ways, this difficulty will be even greater. They can also have particular problems when a group of people are talking together. They will not only have trouble following the content, but may also find it hard to distinguish between voices. This makes following the content of the conversation much more difficult, and what tends to happen is that the person with AS gives up trying and switches off. They become lost in their own thoughts, or distracted by something completely different, and will often re-enter the conversation with a completely unrelated comment.

> *At a family dinner just before Christmas, Frank was sitting with his parents, three brothers and two sets of aunts and uncles. The conversation was lively and discussion ranged from football to favourite films, and then to holidays, and what people were planning for the coming year. Everyone was relaxed and happy, and seemed to be enjoying the party. Frank, however, had long since lost the thread of the conversation, and sat quietly thinking. Suddenly he re-joined the conversation with, 'Which city has more people in it, London or Liverpool?' This completely stopped the flow of conversation, but because the family were used to Frank they just laughed at him.*

Although the other members of his family were used to Frank's odd ways, and thought his interruption funny, it is not difficult to see that anyone who did not know him might see this interruption as odd, and perhaps rather rude. This also has unfortunate consequences for Frank, who even at home gets laughed at, and is not really sure why. In other circumstances people might be less kind.

In this situation, where groups of people are all talking together, it is difficult to give someone with AS a strategy that will help. Their difficulties once again reflect how the brains of those with AS are different. They find it much more difficult to focus their attention, especially when there are lots of things happening at once. They also have difficulty screening out unwanted sounds, so that trying to concentrate on what one person is saying when there is a general background level of conversation can prove impossible.

However, it may help to remind them that they should not interrupt others, if they don't want to be considered rude. Most of us learn early on in life that this is considered rude by others, and by late childhood most children can understand this rule and stick to it, at least some of the time. However, people with AS often find it very difficult to stop themselves interrupting. Sometimes they have never really understood that there is such a rule, and sometimes they just forget, in the heat of wanting to say what they have just thought about. On occasions, they may interrupt because they fear that if they wait they will forget what they needed to say.

In a social skills group for young people, Tim knew that at the beginning of the group each person would be asked what they had done during the week. Tim had had a very exciting week away and could not wait to tell everyone. When he was reminded that he should not interrupt until it was his turn to speak he became very agitated, and despite the reminders he could not stop himself interrupting each new speaker until it was finally his turn. He was upset when told that he was being rude, because he felt that he must tell the others what he had been doing before he forgot.

These characteristics of people with AS make it hard to hold a proper conversation with them. Others see them as rude because they seem not to listen, or they interrupt with something irrelevant. They also tend to talk endlessly about their special interest, and fail to see that they are being boring. Not surprisingly, it will not be long before most people give up trying to interact with them.

If you have a family member with AS, or are working with someone who has the condition, the above descriptions will probably sound familiar. It may help you to cope if you can remind yourself that this is not deliberate rudeness, but simply a failure to be able to follow what is being said. If you want to interact with the person with AS, then try to make your sentences short and simple, and check back with the person that they have understood. Long, complicated instructions or requests will almost certainly be forgotten.

What to talk about

One of the most difficult aspects of holding a conversation with someone with AS can be their obsession with a particular topic or interest. Once started on their pet subject, many people with AS can bore for England! They will go on and on, at great length and in great detail, completely failing to pick up any hints or cues that the other person is not interested and wants to get away. Indeed, if you try to walk away, you may find yourself followed by the person with AS, still talking. People who care for those with AS can find this very wearing and irritating. It can also lead to the person being actively avoided by others.

> Sam loved football cards. He had a huge collection of them, some that he had bought, and some which had been sent to him. They came from all over the world, and at the

least sign of encouragement, Sam would approach some-
one and begin to show them some of his collection, talking
in detail about each one. When a new visitor or carer
arrived, they would often be charmed by Sam's attention,
and would look at his cards with interest. However, they
would soon realize their mistake. Sam would return at
frequent intervals and go through the same cards, with the
same commentary, over and over again. It would not be
long before the new person was avoiding Sam like every-
one else. Sam found this puzzling and hurtful. He felt he
was being friendly, and could not understand why people
soon avoided him.

There are several reasons why this kind of behaviour persists, even though it clearly is not working very well for Sam,
or those around him. People with AS often have difficulty
knowing how to start and maintain a conversation. They find
it hard to know what to say and, because of the difficulty
of attention mentioned above, they have problems keeping
it going once started. Talking about their favourite special
interest solves this problem for them. Because they have spent
hours learning about this area, and going over and over it, the
subject has been well learned. Moreover, because they know
so much about the topic, they can just keep on talking. The
other person gets no chance to reply, so the person with AS
does not have to struggle to remember what they say.

Sadly, of course, this fails as a conversational strategy,
because the other person feels ignored and alienated by such
behaviour. The person with AS, because they are not very
good at processing feedback from others, will often not realize that it is their own behaviour that is causing others to
avoid them. They are more likely to attribute this to the other
person being rude or unkind.

Sometimes people with AS will adopt another strategy, whereby they have a 'standard' conversational opener which never changes. This is more likely to happen with those of limited ability, and it can be unnerving for the recipient. The person with AS will usually ask a series of questions and will pay little attention to the replies. What the other person says is unlikely to change the content of their questions. The effect can be very odd, but clearly the person with AS has some idea of holding a conversation, and is doing the best they can:

Colin: *What is your name?*

New carer: *Robert.*

Colin: *Where do you live?*

New carer: *Epsom.*

Colin: *Have you got any brothers or sisters?*

New carer: *Yes, I have two brothers and one sister.*

Colin: *Will you be here tomorrow?*

New carer: *Yes, I'll see you then.*

On the face of it, there is nothing wrong with this conversation. However, when Robert, the new carer, arrives the next day, he may be surprised to find that he has the same conversation with Colin as he did on this occasion. Colin does not know how to change or maintain a conversation once he has made contact with someone, so he goes through the same routine again.

Changing of topics

At the other extreme from dominating a conversation with a single topic, the person with AS may suddenly change the topic without warning. This can be both confusing and disconcerting for the listener. Usually this is because the person has made a link between the topics in their own mind, but has failed to make that known to the listener. The person with AS will not understand that the person they are talking to is not aware of what they are thinking about. Once again they will have failed to realize how it feels to be 'in someone else's shoes'. Occasionally this can happen because the person has been distracted by something in the environment and feels driven to comment on it. On other occasions it may simply be because their attention has wandered, as in the example of Frank above.

However, despite this tendency to suddenly change topic, the person with AS may strongly dislike the topic being changed when they are talking about something of interest to them. They find this very disconcerting, because the conversation has gone in a direction for which they were unprepared. They may persist in trying to return to their own topic, effectively ignoring what has been said to them. This can also appear rude and inconsiderate to others, and adds to their social difficulties.

These are difficult problems to solve because, in order to help the person with AS develop better conversational skills, they have to be able to overcome a series of problems:

1. finding a topic for the conversation which is appropriate to the other person

2. being able to stop and listen to their reply

3. understanding their reply and remembering the important parts of it

4. responding to it in a way that is appropriate to the other person

5. keeping this going to make a 'real' conversation.

For someone who has problems with attention and short-term memory, as well as some difficulty in understanding, the above set of requirements can be a real challenge. Furthermore, the person with AS may have trouble knowing whether what they are saying is appropriate or not. They find it very hard to judge non-verbal feedback from other people that might signal, for example, that they are bored, embarrassed or annoyed by what the person with AS is saying.

Strategies to help

People with AS can sometimes benefit from specific social skills training to address this kind of problem and give them ideas for starting and maintaining a conversation (more on this at the end of this chapter). However, it is not possible to cure the difficulties of attention and short-term memory, and so the person with AS is always going to be at a disadvantage in a conversational setting. If you are having difficulty in communicating with someone with AS, you do need to be aware of the need to keep things short and simple. It is also wise to check that they have really heard and understood. Some people with AS will adopt a strategy of nodding and smiling as though they understand when they don't, or replying 'Yes' to every question in the hope that the person will just go away and leave them alone.

It may help to give them the idea that any conversation needs to operate rather like a game of tennis. If the game is going to work, both parties have to be able to contribute, and it cannot be all one-sided. This idea can help some people. However, conversations are unpredictable and do not follow a set pattern, and people with AS are not good at dealing with the unpredictable. They like to have rules and routines to follow, as we have already seen. If you are having a conversation with someone with AS, it may help to remind them of the one important rule that both parties need to play a part.

One strategy to suggest may be that they try and remember one detail about the person that they have been talking to, and ask about that the next time they meet. We all use this strategy, and it is a way of making people feel you are interested in them, because you have remembered what they said last time. In the example above, Colin might remember that Robert has two brothers, so the next time they meet he could ask, 'What are your brothers' names?' or 'What do your brothers do for a living?'

It might also help to draw up a list of topics which might be 'safe' topics when meeting someone for the first time. These might be the weather, what they watched on TV last night (as long as this isn't their special interest), the place they are in at the time, or other people that they both know. You may be able to rehearse with the person with AS how a conversation might go, and what kinds of things people might say. It can also be helpful to teach them to use open-ended questions such as 'What do you do for a living?' although you will need to stress that they need to try to listen to the answer, and not jump in with their own account straight away.

Another useful strategy can be to encourage the person with AS to admit that they have trouble remembering what has been said. They might ask the person to repeat what they have said, if it was particularly long or complicated. If asking for instructions, they might ask the person to write it down for them. Often people are embarrassed to admit that they have a problem, or indeed may not really understand what their difficulty is. Helping them to make sense of this, and have some idea of what they can do to overcome it, can be very reassuring.

Another useful technique to teach is how to end a conversation. Sometimes people may carry on talking simply because they cannot work out how to end the conversation. They may just walk away, which only adds to the impression of rudeness. Teaching a few simple phrases such as, 'Well, I must be going now,' or 'I need to go and get a drink now,' can be very helpful.

The extent to which people with AS can remember and make use of such techniques will vary greatly. Less able people with the condition may find it very difficult to remember anything they have been taught, and will often need constant reminders. Those who are more able may learn to make use of simple strategies such as those above to help the social wheels turn a little more smoothly. However, some people, whatever their level of ability, will either be unable or unwilling to alter their behaviour, and in this case those around them will simply have to try to accommodate to them.

Managing conversations

If the person with AS is unwilling or unable to change, then the only way to cope with the conversational difficulties is to develop your own strategies to manage them. This may require you to behave in ways that feel rude to you. However, the person with AS will not pick up subtle hints or cues, so you will have to be direct and open with them:

- Keep things short and simple – be direct and say exactly what you mean. Do not hint; they will not pick up hints.

- Put a limit on a conversation as soon as it starts – if someone approaches you and you know that the conversation will be a long and detailed account of their special interest, you might begin by saying that you can only talk to them for five minutes and then must go.

- Remind them of the need to listen carefully and not interrupt – try to make your reminders gentle and kind, but firm. If you try to do this regularly, the person may begin to remember for themselves.

- Rehearse new situations in advance – when there is a new situation coming up, it may help to role-play the event and try to teach the person with AS what they need to do and say. This can help to reduce anxiety as well.

Talking to yourself

People with AS often talk to themselves. This can lead others to think they are, at best, odd or, at worst, actually mad. However, this habit may simply be a way of rehearsing what they need to remember. We have already seen that remembering things is a problem. Sometimes people seem to use this as a way of rehearsing what they are going to say, or even as a problem-solving strategy.

Sometimes people with AS seem to find it comforting to talk to themselves. Those who live alone may feel it provides company, while others say that it helps reassure them that they can still talk, especially if they spend a lot of time alone. It may be possible to encourage the person to 'think rather than speak' in order to remember things, but they may find it difficult to remember to do this! If they really can't help themselves, you may be able to encourage them to whisper to themselves rather than speak aloud.

Of course, many people do talk to themselves when alone. Unfortunately, people with AS do not seem to be able to stop doing this when others are around. This is not surprising given the difficulty they have in seeing how things may appear to someone else. They will usually have no idea that such behaviour singles them out. Sadly, it makes their difference very obvious to others, and can lead to bullying and exploitation. Someone that I worked with was followed home and sexually propositioned, after somebody had spotted him wandering along happily talking to himself. Fortunately, he knew of the need to be wary of strangers and did not let the man into his house. Another person that I knew was less fortunate, and the person entered his house with him and, although he was not physically harmed, the person stole some of his belongings.

Saying what you think

Most people would probably agree that saying what you think is a good idea. 'Better to be honest,' they say. Unfortunately, if you look at how people behave, most of us do not actually say what we think. We often tell what we call 'white lies' either to save face or to avoid being unkind. If someone asks you 'Does my bum look big in this?' you will probably not tell them the truth, for fear of upsetting them.

People with AS have no such inhibitions. They have little awareness of how the other person may feel about their answer, and assume that if someone asks then they want an honest answer. Moreover, they will sometimes comment spontaneously on another person's appearance, without thinking how this may feel for the other person. Yet again, this can cause social difficulties, and alienate people.

> *John was always interested in new carers who came to work in the supported living hostel where he lived. One day there was a new person who was very overweight. John found this curious and, as soon as he could, he approached her and said, 'Hello, I am John. Why are you so fat?'*

Occasionally it may not be the content which seems offensive, but the tone of voice. We have already noted that the person with AS may have difficulties in regulating their tone of voice and at times they may say something that seems unnecessarily aggressive or blunt. It is rare that there is any intention to be offensive, but others may not realize this and be hurt, or respond aggressively in return.

Another aspect of the same difficulty is the tendency to ask inappropriately personal questions. This can be embarrassing for people who are in a professional role, and thus perhaps less prepared for such a question. However, even family members might be wrong-footed by being asked, 'Is your husband good at sex?' This may be just simple curiosity, but sometimes people with AS will ask personal questions with the intention of discovering whether you are a possible sexual partner for them. Young men with AS are often desperate for a sexual relationship and their conversation will be focused on finding out about sex, and who is likely to be available. Thus 'Have you got a boyfriend?', when addressed to their new young female care worker, will often be the first step to finding out if this person might be a possible target for their affections.

It is wise, if you are in the position of being a paid carer, to be wary of such questions, and to be prepared with a gentle but non-committal answer that you feel comfortable with. While not wishing to be unkind, it is important to nip such ideas in the bud early on, in order to avoid later problems. Some people with AS have been known to become obsessed with a particular person, and this can lead to stalking. While this problem is not common, it can be unnerving, and occasionally dangerous. It is sensible not to risk setting up any unrealistic expectations from the start.

Obtaining information

There will be occasions when you need to ask a person with AS for some kind of account of themselves. As a professional person, you may need to compile a history or file about the person and their difficulties. If you are to achieve your aim, you will need to be very organized and careful. People with AS find it very difficult to give a coherent account of anything in detail. They have great difficulty in marshalling their thoughts and putting them into any clear order. Their difficulties with sequencing will become acutely obvious, and they will interchange things that happened last week and things that happened ten years ago without warning. Their sense of time and how a sequence of events happened over time is often very confused, and they will not be able to give you a coherent account of their life story. Indeed they may not be able to give you a coherent account of what happened to them yesterday.

If you need to get a sequential account from someone with AS, you will need to ask a series of careful and simple questions to find out what you need to know. One of the problems with this is that you may need to ask what appear to be leading questions to get your answers. For example, if you ask someone with AS 'Tell me about your time at school,' they will be unlikely to have any idea of what you want to know. Either they will answer with a brief 'I don't remember,' or you will hear a long, rambling and disconnected series of events, which they will tell you in the vain hope that some of it will be what you want.

On the other hand, it may concern you to have to ask, 'Were you bullied at school?' because you will probably feel you are asking a leading question, to which the answer can all too easily be 'Yes', even if that were not true. The person may say 'Yes' simply because that is easier, and will make you give up questioning them, rather than because they wish to deceive you. This can be a real worry if you need to gain reliable information from the person, as a witness, for example.

If you are faced with this kind of problem, careful planning is needed. You will need to make your questions specific enough that the person can understand them, and feels able to answer you, but not so specific that you appear to be leading them. In the above example you might ask, 'How did the teachers treat you at school? Were they nice or nasty?' When the person has given you their answer, you might then ask, 'What about the other students? Were they nice or nasty to you?' followed perhaps by 'What did they do?'

This approach will obviously take a lot of time and preparation, but you will obtain a much more truthful picture of the person's history than if you just ask them to tell you about their schooldays. You may even need to return to the topic later, and check it out. You might ask later on, 'Did all the students treat you badly, or were some of them friendly?' In addition to breaking down your questions like this, you need to leave time for the person to process and make sense of what you are asking. Do not try to hurry them, or you will not get accurate information.

Social skills training

Many children who are now diagnosed with AS are fortunate enough to get some kind of specialist teaching. They may also have opportunities to be taught social skills, so that they grow into adults with some awareness of their difficulties, and some strategies for managing these. While these strategies do not get rid of the problems altogether, they do mean that the person has some idea of the difficulties that they have, and ways that they can cope.

For those who have AS but have never been diagnosed, or who have only recently received a diagnosis, these experiences will not have been available. Nor will they have had the benefit of parents, teachers or others who understood their difficulties as they grew up. Sadly they are likely to have few opportunities to learn these skills as an adult, even if they are willing and able. Very often their difficulties have been magnified by repeated experiences of failure, bullying and ridicule. Not surprisingly this often makes people withdraw from others, and be very suspicious of those they do not know.

As someone who cares for a person with AS, you may be able to help. You can make explicit attempts to teach them, for example, how to start a conversation, how to maintain it and how to end it. You may also be able to help them learn about non-verbal signals and how these can indicate how someone is feeling. You may be able to teach them to listen to others, and try to control their interruptions. All of these are important verbal skills, but the person with AS will not have learned them, as most of us do, from experience. We have rarely been taught such things explicitly, but have just picked them up as we went along. People with AS will not have done this, because of their particular problems. If they are going to learn, it will be from careful and explicit teaching.

What to teach

- How to start a conversation – simple and safe questions to ask, such as 'Where do you come from?' or 'How was your journey?'

- Listening skills – the need to wait until someone has finished, and then to respond to what they have said, rather than just saying what you want to say. People with AS may find this very hard to do, even when they are trying their best.

- How to make sympathetic comments – if someone tells the person that something unfortunate has happened, to say something like, 'Oh dear, poor you,' or 'That must have been annoying.'

- Techniques to 'repair' a conversation – questions such as, 'Sorry I didn't quite understand. What did you say?'

- Polite ways to end a conversation – 'I must be going now, my tea is ready,' or 'Nice to meet you. See you again soon.'

- Inoffensive ways to make conversation with someone you fancy as a sexual partner – the old favourite, 'Do you come here often?' or remarks such as 'I really like this music, don't you?'

- Making links – how to make someone aware of the connection between two topics, when you want to change from one to the other. For example, 'That reminds me of something I saw on TV last night.'

- Giving and receiving compliments gracefully – saying 'Thank you' if someone makes a complimentary remark, rather than brushing it off or ignoring it. Telling someone they look nice, when you want to develop the friendship.

- Asking for help – being brave enough to say, 'I don't know,' or 'Can you help me with this?' if confused or uncertain.

Even then, many adults with AS will probably find it hard to change their behaviour. It is generally easier to shape the behaviour of a child or young person than it is an adult. When someone has been how they are for forty years or more, it is going to be very difficult for them to change, even if they want to. Their patterns of behaviour will be well learned, and often adults resent the expectation that they should change. You will have to be guided by the person themselves. If they seem troubled by their difficulties, it can be helpful to explore these issues with them, and suggest approaches like those above as possible solutions. However, some people will have been so hurt and distressed by their early experiences that they have lost all motivation to try to fit in, and their strategy will often be that of withdrawal into fierce independence, regardless of how they seem to others to be struggling.

SUMMARY

o The language of those with AS can be unusual in terms of both content and expression.

o People with AS have difficulty starting and maintaining conversations except when they are talking about their special interests.

o People with AS have particular difficulty in following a conversation which is taking place in a group, between several people, because of their problems of attention and memory.

o People with AS tend to interrupt and abruptly change the subject, usually because they have lost track of what others are saying and are absorbed in their own thoughts.

o People with AS may seem abrupt or rude, because they often say what they are thinking without considering its effect on others.

o The tone of voice of a person with AS may sound aggressive when this is not intended.

o The performance of people with AS in conversation can be improved by specific teaching, but they will always have some difficulties in this area.

Chapter 6

Social Rules and Relationships

We have already noted that people with Asperger syndrome often have problems with social situations. Unlike people with autism they usually want to achieve a degree of social success, but often fail to do so. Many people with AS express a wish to have friends or a sexual partner, while those with autism are more often quite happy alone. However, like people with autism, those with AS have difficulty 'putting themselves into someone else's shoes'. They lack what has been called a 'theory of mind'.

Most of us can imagine, to some extent, how it would feel to be someone else. Indeed, this is often a large part of our early socialization. If, as a child, I steal my brother's chocolate, my mother may ask, 'How would you like it if I took your chocolate?' I am asked to imagine the situation and see what it would feel like. Most of us can do this to a greater or lesser degree quite early in childhood. As we get older, we get more sophisticated about it. Watching a tragic movie, we cry for the heroine, or are happy for the hero. We can imagine how it feels to be that person.

People with Asperger syndrome find this extremely difficult to do. They are stuck at a stage of development where they see the world from their own perspective, and only from their own perspective. They cannot imagine how it feels to be someone else. One of the effects of this is that they can appear very selfish. They will act in ways which meet their own needs, but completely fail to see how what they do may affect others. They may get very hurt and angry at the behaviour of other people towards them, and attribute all kinds of malicious intent to them, while completely failing to see that they may be doing something similar to those around them.

People with AS do not understand that other people have needs and wants like their own, and they will do whatever seems best for them, without considering how this might affect those around them. An example might be playing music late into the night because they are unable to sleep, and failing to understand that this will keep others awake and annoy them. If others complain, they will see that as being unreasonable and probably feel that the person who is complaining has a grudge against them.

You may be able to improve the social skills of the person with AS, if you can teach them some of the basic rules about social interaction. One simple rule that may help is to introduce the idea that friendships need to be reciprocal. If someone does something for you, then you should try and do something in return, though not always immediately. It may help to talk to the person about those who are close to them, and about what those people like and do not like. You could introduce the idea that doing something that a person likes will be a way to make them happy, and will encourage them to like you more. People with AS will often have great trouble appreciating what someone else might like for a gift, for example, and without some guidance may give the other person something that they themselves would like instead.

This can sometimes seem amusing, but it can be hurtful and upsetting for the person on the receiving end, who may feel that the person with AS is being insensitive and selfish.

> *Chris loved trains. He knew all the old steam trains, the different types and their names. He knew the routes that each ran on, and the names of the companies that operated each line. When it was his mother's birthday, he bought her a book about trains. His mum did not know whether to laugh or cry!*

If you cannot 'put yourself into someone else's shoes', it is impossible to understand how what you do might affect someone else. In the example above, Chris imagined that because he likes trains, then his mother must do also. He cannot imagine how it feels to be his mother, or what kinds of things might please her instead.

This difficulty will also make it hard to see how another person might feel if something bad happens in their life. Thus someone with AS may laugh if someone has an accident, or appear indifferent when told of a bereavement. This type of apparently unkind and insensitive response can make people with AS disliked by others. However, their response is rarely malicious in intent, it simply reflects their inability to see how it might feel to be someone else.

In a worst case, this can lead to truly antisocial behaviour which brings the person with AS into conflict with the law. For example, someone might commit a sexual assault, simply because their sexual needs are overpowering at that instant, and they cannot see how their behaviour might affect their victim. Because sexual contact is pleasant and exciting for them, they assume that the same is true for their victim. We have also seen that people with AS find it difficult to process feedback and learn from experience, so they may repeat the undesirable behaviour despite clear feedback that it is not acceptable.

> *Dennis has been in trouble with the law several times. He likes to watch young girls in the local playground, and on several occasions has approached them. Twice he tried to kiss, touch and cuddle a girl, and each time this resulted in a visit from the police, and an appearance in court. When this happened for the third time, Dennis found himself locked in a secure hospital, with the label of 'sex-offender'. Dennis still does not understand what he did wrong.*

At a less serious level, this failure to see another person's point of view can lead to other forms of 'offensive' behaviour. As we have seen, the person with AS will fail to understand what another person is likely to think or feel, so they will not be able to think, for example, 'If I say that, this person may be offended.' Thus their tendency is to say whatever comes into their mind: 'Gosh you have got a big nose!' or 'Why don't you cut your hair?'

While such comments can seem childlike or endearingly funny in some situations, they can also cause great offence or hurt. The person with AS is likely to be unaware that what they say is inappropriate, and may not realize they have upset someone unless that person becomes really angry or offensive in return. Even if this happens they may not associate the response with their own behaviour but simply see the other person as being aggressive and nasty.

This tendency to say what they think means that people with AS are often brutally honest, and there are times when honesty is an admirable quality. However, most of us learn to be a bit more circumspect in telling others exactly what we think. It does not oil the social wheels and can lead to anger, hostility and rejection. The problem for those with

AS is that they usually fail to realize that they have upset the other person, and will not understand why they have reacted as they have.

Despite their honesty in saying what they think about other people, most people with AS dislike being criticized themselves. If you are going to provide feedback about their social failures, you will need to be tactful and gentle in doing it. Most adults with AS will have had many, many experiences of getting things wrong, being laughed at, being teased or bullied for being different, and as a result they are often very sensitive to any comments about their social performance.

Social rules

Social situations are governed by a complicated series of social rules. Most of us learn these social rules as we grow up, often without ever being explicitly told what they are. We watch others, and we find out when what we are doing is not acceptable, sometimes by being told off, but often simply by picking up that others are not pleased with our behaviour. Most children are tuned into their parents' wishes and feelings, and want to please them, so that any expression of disapproval will usually be noticed and remembered. Even if we choose to ignore parents' wishes, it will not be long before other people in society will make it clear that our behaviour is not acceptable.

People with AS are very poor at picking up such feedback from others. They often fail to recognize the non-verbal cues that most of us respond to. Even when the feedback is quite explicit, like being shouted at or even hit, they may still not be able to make the link between their own behaviour and the outcome. They will usually think that the other person is just being unkind.

It is possible to help the person with AS make better sense of social situations by making these rules more explicit. However, you will need to spell things out very clearly and sometimes bluntly, if they are going to be able to learn. Social situations are very complicated. There are unwritten rules about personal space, touching, what you can and cannot say, what you do and do not do, as well as a whole raft of complicated rules about interacting with a possible sexual partner. Once you are in a close relationship, there is another set of rules about what is acceptable in that situation, and what is not.

Personal space

When you begin talking to someone, it is usual to maintain a certain physical distance between you. This varies in different countries and different cultures, but in the UK it is usually about two to three feet. If you are intimate with someone, or know them very well, this distance may be smaller. With those who we have just met, or who are casual acquaintances, the distance will be slightly greater. If you stand too close or too far away, others will find this uncomfortable, even though they may not express it openly.

> *Jonathan always liked to stand very close to anyone that he was talking to. He did not realize that this made many people feel uncomfortable. One day, when waiting for a train to go to work, he got talking to an elderly lady who was also waiting. As they chatted, Jonathan got closer and closer to her, and she began to feel quite frightened of him. In the end she complained to one of the station staff who threatened to call the police if Jonathan did not leave her alone. Jonathan could not understand her reaction. He thought he was just being friendly.*

People with AS are not usually aware of these rules about personal space, and it is not uncommon to find that they stand much closer to other people than is usual. If this happens, the person they are standing near will usually move away a little. This is not usually a conscious decision, but something that has become automatic. The person with AS may then move nearer again, and the other person moves back, so that they end up being pursued by the person with AS.

From a distance, this kind of interaction may look amusing, but it will feel very uncomfortable for the person who is being pursued. Generally we tend to stand closer to people that we know well, or to those in whom we have sexual interest, so this kind of behaviour from a stranger can feel quite threatening. Not surprisingly it can be yet another reason why the person with AS finds that others avoid them in social situations.

If you want to teach people to observe this kind of social distance, you will have to be quite specific. One simple technique is to get them to stretch out their arm and just touch the other person with their fingertips. This will give them a reasonably acceptable social distance to work with, and can be practised at home until they have a feel for the correct kind of distance. However, it is probably not a good idea to practise this with strangers!

Another way is to tell the person quite explicitly, by saying something like, 'If you stand that close to me, it makes me feel very uncomfortable. Please move further back.' If they do not move back far enough, you might then try the above fingertip technique to give them a good idea of a reasonable distance. This can take a lot of practice to get right, and you may have to explain several times that it makes people anxious if someone that they do not know stands too close. Most people with AS can relate to the idea of anxiety very well, as it is a big problem for them, so that may help them begin to have some idea of why people dislike this invasion of space.

Touching

If standing too close can feel threatening, then inappropriate touching can feel even more so. If someone that we do not know comes and touches us, our response may vary from surprise to fear, or even anger, depending on how and where they touch, and who they are. We are less likely to feel threatened by a touch from a child or an elderly person, for example.

Touch can be simply a way of gaining attention, or it may be affectionate. However, it can also carry sexual or aggressive overtones, and thus the touch of a stranger can be very alarming. If the touch is on a part of the body usually associated with sexual contact, such as breast or buttocks, we may respond with fear or anger, or both. As with social rules in general, there are very strict, but usually unspoken, rules about who you can touch, when and where. Some of these rules are upheld by the law. People with AS may be unaware of these rules or, at best, hazy about them. This can put them at risk of being misunderstood, and even of being arrested and locked up, if they make a mistake.

It is important therefore, if you are trying to help someone with AS, that you teach them about the most important rules of touch. It is not acceptable to touch a woman's breasts, for example, unless you are her sexual partner (or perhaps a medical person). This is a clear and important rule to teach. Touching her buttocks may cause less outrage, but can still get one into trouble with the law, if she complains. Similarly, touching a man's penis will get you into trouble unless you are his sexual partner, and touching his buttocks will probably do so as well. Some men may respond violently to such touches, even if they do not complain to the police, so the person doing the touching is putting themselves at risk too.

Touching someone's arm, in contrast, is not so likely to cause offence, or get one into serious trouble, even though a stranger may be surprised or alarmed by such a move.

It is very important that people with AS understand that many of these rules about touch are upheld by the law. It is not a defence, for example, to say that they wanted the person to be their sexual partner. While that may be true, the person being touched needs to also have agreed to the physical contact. People with AS, especially young men in the grip of their hormones, may make the mistake of thinking that this kind of touching is a way to approach a potential sexual partner, and can get themselves into serious trouble in consequence. If the opportunity is available for more detailed social skills training, teaching people about who it is OK to touch, and where, can avoid a lot of problems in the future. Consider the following differences:

Family member: You can touch the arms, legs, hands, feet or head, and body apart from breasts, sexual parts and buttocks. You can hug or kiss them.

Sexual partner: You can probably touch any part, but you should be certain they do not object. However, the time and place chosen for this touching needs to be considered. The partner may object to being touched intimately in public, for example, or when they are busy with a task.

Child: You can only touch children who you are related to, or know very well, and then only with their parents' consent, and not on the buttocks or sexual parts. You might hug or kiss a child, but similarly only if you know them well, or are related to them, and have both the child's and their parents' consent.

Friend: You may hug or kiss a friend, but usually only if you know them well. You may touch hands, arms, shoulders and back, but probably no other parts.

Stranger: You would probably only touch hands or arms. You might put an arm around them if they were hurt or distressed.

Doctor or nurse: A doctor or nurse may touch people in ways that would be called intimate if the purpose was not medical.

It is hardly surprising that some people with AS find this confusing. However, this is perhaps one of the most important sets of social rules that they need to know, if they are not to get into serious trouble. It may also be important to explain that the rules are different for doctors and others who are trying to help us, or you may find there are problems if the person with AS has to go to the doctor or into hospital.

Eye contact

The degree of eye contact that we make with someone is another very important social message, which is associated with particular rules. If we make too much eye contact, we are staring, and staring may be interpreted as aggressive, curious, sexual or dominating, depending on who we are staring at and where. If we make too little eye contact, we may be labelled shy, bored, uninterested, dishonest or untrustworthy. Trying to talk to someone whose eye contact is not what we usually expect can feel very uncomfortable. Try having a conversation with someone who steadfastly looks away from you. You will probably 'dry up' surprisingly quickly!

If you watch two people having a conversation in a normal setting, you may notice that they are involved in a kind of social dance. Their eye contact will constantly change and will be complementary. As one person starts to speak they look at the other, then look away. When they look again, this is usually the signal for the other person to reply. The one who is listening looks more intently at their partner, and if this does not happen the speaker will feel that they are not listening. In addition to the eye contact, their body posture will also change, and they will often mirror each other. All of this is unconscious. If you start to think about how you do it, you will become very self-conscious, and probably won't be able to do it normally. It is like the old story of the centipede who ran downstairs quite easily until someone asked him how he did it. When he thought about it, he fell down the stairs!

The complex, and unconscious nature of this kind of interaction makes it very hard to teach people with AS how to manage their eye contact more effectively. However, there are simple rules that you can teach that may help. One is the rule about looking at someone who is speaking. Many people with AS find this difficult. They seem to find eye contact somewhat overwhelming. A good strategy, if this is the case, is to suggest that they look at the other person's mouth or nose instead. Even when they understand the idea, they may still find it difficult to remember to look at someone. If they really feel that they cannot do this, you may be able to teach them to say something such as 'I find it hard to look at people, but I am listening to you.'

The other extreme of eye contact is to stare at other people. This can cause other problems. Some young men, in particular, will take great exception to being stared at, and the person with AS may find themselves the focus of real aggression. Persistent eye contact or staring can also signal sexual interest, and if the person with AS is a young man staring at someone else's girlfriend, he may again find himself in trouble. A woman who is stared at may feel uncomfortable or threatened.

Try to encourage someone who is inclined to stare to look away every so often, or to make a point of looking out of the window, or at their hands. A simple rule like this may save them from a lot of difficulty. It will initially take a lot of practice, and may be hard to achieve, but with lots of gentle reminders it may be possible to moderate their staring into a more acceptable form.

The use of eye contact in making sexual relationships can be fraught with difficulty. Initial interest in someone is often signalled by eye contact, and it can be a central part of flirting and early courtship. Again the rules are complicated and probably impossible to teach. Essentially, a lot of eye contact, followed by sudden aversion of the eyes if the other person looks back, can be a signal of interest, but this is not likely to be noticed by the average person with AS. They may give inadvertent signs of interest to others when they are not interested, which can cause difficulties, or they may appear invasive and even predatory if they stare at people that they are interested in.

If you are trying to help someone with AS in this area, you will probably only be able to teach them the simplest of strategies for managing their eye contact, and you may be able to help them to be aware that there are other messages involved. However, they will probably find it difficult to use this information to change their own behaviour significantly. The major problem will be that they will forget to do it at the appropriate time. It is such an automatic process that it is difficult to change. Try changing your own level of eye contact when talking to a friend, and see what happens. Warn them first though, or they may think you are behaving very oddly.

Making friends

The majority of people with AS have trouble making and keeping friends. So far we have defined the following as areas of difficulty for the person with AS:

- personal hygiene
- language and understanding
- conversational skills
- use of personal space
- eye contact.

Odd or unsatisfactory performance in any or all of these areas may put other people off making friends with the person with AS. In addition, their difficulties with theory of mind, or 'putting themselves in someone else's shoes', may mean that they can often appear selfish and thoughtless. Consequently, even if they cope with all the above, and do make contact with someone as a possible friend, they may still ultimately lose the friendship because they fail to behave as a satisfactory friend to the other person.

Because of these difficulties in making real friends, it is not uncommon to find that someone with AS will acquire a 'friend' who is actually out to exploit them. The person with AS will be very grateful to find someone who seems to take an interest in them, and will not see that they are being exploited. This 'friend' may exploit them financially or sexually, and this can often happen without the person with AS really understanding what is going on. Those around them, such as family members or professional carers, may see what is happening but be powerless to intervene, because what is happening is all with the person's consent. This can be both frustrating and distressing for those who care about the person with AS.

Peter was a young man with AS. He was taken to a night-club by some of his former schoolmates, and while there was approached by a young woman who clearly found him sexually attractive. Peter was highly flattered, and by the end of the evening this young woman was keen to come home with him. By the following weekend she had moved into his flat, and for several weeks remained there, spending his money and eating his food. Peter was so delighted to have a girlfriend and a sexual relationship for the first time in his life, that he would not listen when his friends tried to tell him that she was only after his money. However, sure enough, when his bank account was empty, she quickly tired of him and moved on. Peter was devastated, and deeply hurt.

Unfortunately, as the law currently stands it is impossible for family or friends to intervene in such situations. If the exploitation is happening with the person's consent, nothing can be done, unless you can prove that they do not have the intellectual ability to be responsible for their own affairs. Usually they will not thank you for interfering.

From friends to lovers

Most people want to have a long-term sexual partner, and many people with AS are no different. Young men with AS may be particularly desperate to be like other young men, and have a girlfriend and a sexual relationship. Of course, as with the rest of the population, for some it will be a same-sex partner rather than opposite sex, and it is important not to make assumptions about this. Whatever the sex of the partner, however, the step from friend to sexual partner can be fraught with difficulty.

Most of us find the social rules around establishing a sexual relationship confusing and difficult at times, especially when we are young. The rules that govern how you approach someone you fancy, how you judge whether your feelings are returned, how you develop and maintain the relationship, and what is acceptable within the relationship are extremely complicated. They vary from age group to age group, and between cultures and races. If most of us find them complicated, it is not too difficult to see that people with AS, with all their other problems in this area, can find these rules almost impossible to negotiate.

When trying to help someone in this area of life, the two most important things to teach are how to approach someone appropriately (and thus not get into trouble with the law) and safe ways to meet others who may become either friends or sexual partners in due course. Some people with AS will choose the most unsuitable places to meet people and thereby put themselves at risk.

> *Philip decided that the best place to meet a girlfriend would be at the local supermarket. He often went there with his mother to shop, and he knew that lots of women of all ages went there too. One day he took the bus alone and went to the supermarket to search for a likely person. He soon saw a young woman he fancied. Philip waited until she left the shop and then followed her home. He could not understand why she seemed alarmed by this and threatened to call the police.*

Sometimes people with AS will put themselves at risk of assault, without realizing the danger. Their lack of awareness of social rules can make them very vulnerable.

Susie loved to spend the evening in her local pub. She would dress up in her best clothes, looking quite alluring with a low neckline and high heels. One evening, she was sitting at the bar, showing lots of leg, and chatting to the barman who knew her well. Eventually she said loudly to him, in hearing of a number of men who were standing at the bar, 'I am looking for a boyfriend. Do you know anyone who wants a girlfriend?'

If you know someone who might be at risk of these kinds of behaviour, it is important to try to teach them some basic social rules about what is and is not OK in such situations. As with children and young people, you will need to teach them explicitly about keeping safe.

It may also be helpful to spend some time thinking of places they might go to meet others more safely. These might be clubs, sports classes or events, or organizations such as religious groups or charities, where they are less likely to meet those who will exploit them. It may be possible to find a club which is linked to a special interest that they have, which can then serve two purposes for them.

Bear in mind though, when you are discussing these matters with someone with AS, that you will have to be very direct and blunt with them. It is no use saying vaguely, 'That isn't a very good idea.' You will need to spell out exactly why, and at times you will need to express yourself in a way that may feel rude to you. If someone's personal hygiene is poor, you will have to say something like, 'If you don't have a bath every day, and put on clean clothes, you will soon smell horrible, and nobody will want to talk to you.'

Although this may sound unkind, if you say it gently and kindly, then the message will not usually be taken as an insult. Often someone with AS will not have seriously thought about this matter. They do not mind how they smell, so they assume that nobody else will either, if indeed they think about it at all.

In the case of behaviour like Susie's above, you may have great difficulty in spelling out why her behaviour could get her into trouble. You may find that her understanding of sexual signals is minimal, and she will have no idea when she might be at risk of assault, or when someone is genuinely attracted to her. Even if you are able to get such a message across, it is often the case that the person fails to remember at the necessary time. The wish to attract others and be seen as normal will be too strong to ignore. It is not uncommon for young women with AS to be referred to psychology services for such behaviour, in the hope that some sex education may solve the problem. In reality this is rarely the case, for the reasons already given. The best solution is to try to ensure that the person always goes out with someone else, but they may dislike that idea, seeing it as unnecessary interference. This is a difficult problem to resolve and there is no easy answer.

Relationships that work and those that do not

For most people with AS, the relationships that work best are usually those they have with parents and siblings. Even though these can be stormy at times, it is usually the case that these people will, over the years, have come to some understanding of the person's difficulties, and are able to make allowances for them. By a process of trial and error, they will often have worked out what seems to work, and what does not. Even though they may remain puzzled and frustrated by the person with AS, they can usually make some accommodation to their needs.

Of course, parents cannot be around forever, and it is often when parents die that the adult with AS begins to have real problems. If they are fortunate, they may have siblings who will take over where parents left off, but understandably not all siblings feel willing or able to take on this task, and some people will have no other close family.

It is less common that friends will offer a lot of support, because we usually expect a friendship to be reciprocal. In other words we expect to get as well as give. People with AS are not very good at the giving side, because they are often unaware that it is expected, or indeed of how to go about it. Thus anyone who is a friend of someone with AS will often find themselves in a supportive role, where they are giving more than they are getting back. Where friendships endure, it is most often when the people concerned have known each other since childhood, and have grown up together. Like the family members, these kinds of friends will have learned to make allowances.

More usually, adults with AS may say that they were part of a group at school, but that they did not really feel accepted. Rather they were just tolerated. Part of the problem can be that sometimes people with AS can be very demanding as friends, especially when young. They can be possessive, and have fixed ideas about what friends should and should not do, and can, as a result, drive their friends away. Thus for most people with AS it is rare to find that they have a network of supportive friends.

Sometimes, however, people with AS are able to strike up a friendship with someone who has the same condition. This can be very successful, especially if they share a special interest. They will have the same expectations of each other, so that neither is disappointed. However, other difficulties can arise because they will both have the same problem in not knowing how to sustain a friendship, and without support and encouragement may just let it die. This will not usually be because they do not value it, but because they simply do not know how to maintain it. They may need explicit help in learning how to arrange meetings and make phone calls to each other, to keep up the contact. In these days of emails, this may be a preferred approach, as many people with AS like the impersonal distance offered by computers.

Sexual relationships can be more difficult to establish, as we have already seen, and are more risky because of the possibility of exploitation. On the other hand, it can happen that someone with AS will marry and have a family, and live with someone for many years. While these relationships may appear to work, if the AS is unrecognized, as it usually is, then the partner will often have spent many years being hurt, puzzled and frustrated by their AS partner's behaviour. A crisis may occur when they finally feel that they have had enough, and either leave, or threaten to do so.

Occasionally these couples will come for a diagnosis late in life, with the hope that something can be changed. Although a diagnosis can be a huge relief in such situations, because it explains what has been happening, it does not necessarily relieve the problems. The partner may have come to get their other half 'fixed' and, when it becomes apparent that this cannot happen, they may decide to give up on the relationship. Typically this will be a man with AS and a wife who has tried to accommodate to him for years. However, it is also possible that the roles might be reversed.

When such relationships break down, it can be enormously hurtful to both parties. The one who does not have AS feels ignored, neglected and exploited, while the one who does tends to feel hurt, indignant and misunderstood. It is not unusual, when such a breakdown happens, to find that the person with AS becomes depressed or otherwise mentally ill, and appears at their local doctor's surgery asking for help.

Occasionally, as with friendships between those with AS, a person will meet and marry another person who also has

AS. This perhaps offers the best chance of happiness, because each partner is much more likely to understand the other, and will not have the same expectations of emotional support and expressions of affection that a non-AS partner will have. As with many of us, the most successful relationship is with someone who has similar wants, needs and attitudes.

Bullying

We have already noted the risk that those with AS will be victimized and exploited, sexually or financially, and either with or without their consent. While this can be worrying, a more common version of this situation is that of being bullied. The majority of adults with AS will have memories of being bullied at school, and these can be highly distressing. One young man I worked with could not tell me the details of what had been done to him, even after ten years away from school, because he became so tearful and upset when he tried to recall it. Another had been sexually abused at his boarding school, and similarly found it almost impossible to talk about. Bullying can be vicious and damaging, and the effects are long-lasting. It is particularly distressing when the victim cannot understand why it is happening, and for those with AS this is usually the case.

Much of this book is about the differences between those with AS and others, and unfortunately there are many people in our society who feel threatened by those who are different. People may be targeted because of what they wear, how they speak, where they live, because they are too bright or not bright enough, or simply because they look odd. Children are notoriously inclined to pick out anyone different and bully them, but many adults are no better. Unfortunately, if you have been bullied as a child, you tend to be more vulnerable to bullying as an adult too. Bullying damages self-esteem and leaves scars that never really heal without therapeutic help.

People with AS are often easy targets for bullies. They often look and sound different from everyone else, and their lack of understanding of social rules makes them stand out. In addition, they are often easy to wind up, being highly anxious and easily frustrated. Many bullies learn how to wind someone with AS up to the point where they explode and then stand back to watch the fun, as the person with AS gets themselves into trouble.

Bullying is difficult to stop. Many schools struggle with the problem, and sadly bullying is endemic to many work-places. As a person who cares for someone with AS you may be able to approach someone who is in a senior position to ask for action to prevent the bullying. However, this may not work very well and it may be more fruitful to try to teach the person with AS how to be more assertive and resist the bul-lying. If the bullying deteriorates into physical violence, you should involve the police immediately, because this is assault. If the person is seriously distressed by bullying, then it may be necessary to remove them from the situation completely. If necessary, approach their family doctor to ask for a period of sick leave while the situation is reviewed. In some situations, it may help if the person with AS sees a counsellor. However, given the problems with language and communication, this may need to be someone with special skills and experience of AS.

The need to be alone

Many of us feel a need to spend some time alone on occa-sions. For some people this need will be greater than others. For people with AS it may be particularly important. Because social situations are so challenging and demanding for them, they often feel that they need time alone to recover and just be themselves. This is where their special interest can be a great source of comfort. In this area they are knowledgeable and successful. They cannot be a failure because there is no one to judge. This time to regroup and recover is very important, and you should not begrudge the person with AS such time as and when they need it.

Even when being sociable, people with AS may have a different perception of friends and partners than most of us. They may be content with what appear to the rest of us as very superficial relationships. A few minutes or hours together can result in someone being viewed as a good friend, and to maintain the friendship someone with AS may only require a few minutes' contact from time to time. It is as though just being acknowledged can be sufficient.

People with AS find social situations difficult and confusing. We can try to help in all the ways so far outlined, but they are never going to find these situations easy. It is exactly the same feeling as most of us would have if we were suddenly dropped into the middle of a very different culture, such as China or Japan. We would not know the rules, the language would be a mystery, and it would be very easy to say or do the wrong thing. Life for someone with AS is like this all the time while they are trying to cope with the rest of us. It is hardly surprising that they need to escape at times.

Summary

o   People with AS find social situations challenging because they have never learned and do not understand
the rules.

o   Problems with language and memory make the situation
worse, because people with AS find it hard to take part
in conversations and follow what is being said.

o   People with AS may have different expectations of
friends, and may allow others to exploit them because
they are so grateful to have a 'friend'.

o   The desire for a sexual relationship can cause people
with AS to put themselves at risk.

o   It may help to work out some safer and potentially more
successful places to meet people, perhaps in accordance
with one of the person's special interests.

o   Bullying has often been a problem for people with AS
as children, and can continue to be so even when they
are adults.

o   The stresses and strains of coping with social situations
can lead the person with AS to need time alone in order
to recover.

Chapter 7

Problem-solving and Coping with Change

Problem-solving is part of everyday life. We need to be able to 'think on our feet' because situations change, demands change and things go wrong. Most of us can do this reasonably well as adults, because we have faced many problems throughout life and have learned the skills needed. Occasionally we may come up against a new problem, or a particularly complicated one that stumps us. In those situations we may need to ask others for help, but even when this happens, we will usually learn something new from such experiences each time.

People with AS have difficulty with problem-solving. We have already seen that they find it hard to hold and remember verbal information or instructions. They cannot remember everything that is said to them, and can become very anxious because they fear that they will forget. Anxiety tends to make anyone more likely to forget, because it affects concentration, so those with AS have a double problem. They may also fail to learn from earlier experiences.

Think for a moment about how you might deal with a problem that crops up suddenly: imagine you are on your way to work, and time is short. You need to stop at the cashpoint to get some cash, so that you will be able to buy some lunch.

When you get to the cashpoint you discover that it is not working. The next nearest cashpoint is in the opposite direction to your normal journey to work. What will you do?

In order to solve this problem, you will weigh up several possibilities. You might turn round and go to the other cashpoint, but this will make you late for work. You might decide to manage without any cash, and hope that you can borrow enough to buy some lunch, or pay for it using a credit card. Alternatively you might decide to carry on to work, but look for other places to stop along the way that might have a cashpoint.

Each of these possible solutions will have different implications. Being late for work might get you into trouble with your boss. If you have often been late before, it might even lose you your job. Borrowing from a friend might upset the friend, or your friend may not have enough money. Also, if you have often borrowed money from them before, they may not be willing to lend you any more, especially if you have been slow to repay it. You might try to pay by credit card, but you worry that this may be refused. You might already be overspent on your card. If all of these apply, you may feel forced into taking your chances on finding another cashpoint along the way. Or you may have to go without lunch.

People with AS find this kind of task extremely difficult. As you can see from the discussion above, the thought processes that most people would go through in solving a problem like this can be very complicated. There are several strands to it, and each strand has a different outcome. In order to decide what to do, you have to decide which is likely to be the most successful approach for you, with the least negative outcome. While you are working through this task, you are holding a lot of information in your mind at the same time, and weighing each option against the others. Yet your decision-making process may be very rapid. You may work through all these options in two or three minutes at the most, before deciding what to do.

Someone with AS will not usually be able to get much beyond the first strand. One of two things may happen. They may get anxious and distressed and seek help, or they may do the most obvious thing, which may not be the best for them. If they are highly distressed, this might be something like kicking the cash machine, which is likely to get them into trouble. They are very unlikely to be able to think through all the options outlined above.

Most people with AS can appear quite rigid to others. They tend to develop set routines for doing things, and do not vary these, whatever happens. When faced with a new situation where they have no routine, they may simply do nothing. It may not even occur to them to ask for help.

> *Michael had a cash card and a credit card. He was reasonably good at managing his money most of the time, using his cash card to draw money for everyday expenses, and his credit card only for special things such as holidays or large purchases. One day he realized that he had lost his cash card. He decided that he would use his credit card instead. He paid for everything he bought with his credit card, and at the end of the month had accumulated a large debt. When the card statement arrived he was horrified, and did not know what to do. He did not think there would be any money in his bank to pay it, as he had forgotten that he was not drawing any money out with his cash card as usual. In a panic, he threw the bill away.*

Despite being an able person in many ways, Michael's problem-solving skills were poor. He did not think to let the bank know that he had lost his card, and soon forgot that he was not using the money in his bank account in the usual way.

When the bill came, he panicked, and rather than ask for help he just threw it away. This kind of irrational response to problems is not uncommon, and it often makes the problem much worse. People with AS find it very hard to generate alternative solutions to a problem.

Problem-solving is a skill that can be learned, and you may have some success in teaching people with AS some aspects of it. You could encourage them to try 'brain-storming' to come up with as many ideas as they can when given an imaginary problem to solve. Taking each idea in turn, you can then work through these together to see which might work best. However, do not expect that having done this once, they will be able to do it alone. You will need to rehearse possible solutions many times.

What you may be able to do, though, is pre-empt problems. You could imagine a number of different scenarios that might occur, and work through to a possible solution. You might then write these down somewhere safe for the person to look at from time to time – perhaps on a wall chart. Below is a list of common problems that could crop up, together with possible solutions:

Problem	What to do
I lock myself out of the house	Leave a spare key with a neighbour or relative
I lose my credit or cash card	Ring the bank (note the relevant phone number)
My train is cancelled	Ask the counter clerk when there is another one
A water pipe in the house begins to leak	Turn off the stopcock and get help
An electrical item goes bang	Turn off the electricity and get help
A fire breaks out	Leave the house and call the Fire Brigade

Of course this list could be huge, so it may be helpful just to focus on those scenarios which are most likely to put the person at risk, or to cause long-term problems in other ways (like losing a cash or credit card). You could also rehearse this list from time to time. It is important to rehearse the practical parts too, such as turning off the stopcock. This has several benefits. By actually doing the action, someone with AS will be much more likely to remember it. In addition, you can make sure that they know where the stopcock is, and make sure that it is possible to turn it off. With repetition, the person with AS will eventually learn the various solutions, although in the panic of a real situation they may not remember at first. This is where a written reminder can be very helpful. People with AS have much better visual skills than verbal ones, so it may also be helpful to explore more visual ways of problem-solving, such as diagrams or charts with pictures.

Forward planning

Having set routines and ways of doing things offers some protection from the uncertainty of life, but there will always be times when things change, or go wrong. In these circumstances it is important to make sure that the person with AS has a strategy for coping. At best, they may have a trusted family member or friend who they can approach for help. If such a person is not available, then it may be helpful to try to identify someone else that they could turn to when anything goes wrong.

If you are not able to work through a list of strategies as suggested above, or you doubt that the person would be able to take these steps on their own, you might give them a written list of people they can approach if a problem suddenly arises. Of course, there will be people who are more appropriate for certain problems. You could suggest a list such as the doctor for anything health-related, the bank's customer service number for anything money-related, the landlord or landlady for anything related to the place they live, and so on. This may seem obvious, but many people with AS, especially if stressed and upset, will not think of these on their own.

If the person is less able, it may be more successful to use diagrams or pictures to indicate the appropriate person or place to approach. For those who are unlikely to be able to explain clearly what is wrong to a stranger, it will probably be better to try to identify one person who will be a source of advice, if this is at all possible. If you decide to do this, do make sure that the person nominated has a good understanding of AS, and that the person with AS feels comfortable and safe in talking to them.

The effects of change

Life is always unpredictable, and change is inevitable. Many of us dislike change, and prefer to stick to our tried and tested ways. When forced to adapt to new ways of doing things we often complain and feel uneasy. However, most of us are able to adapt reasonably well, given time. We develop new ways and new habits, and after a while we are as comfortable as before.

We also usually like to have a degree of order in our lives, and most people will have their own ways of doing things and their own places to put everyday belongings. We tend to dislike or resent others changing our systems and habits. People with AS are no different, but their need for order can be much stronger than it is for most of us. They may spend a lot of time putting their belongings in certain places or arrangements, and may return to check these from time to time. This helps them to know where things are, and to find what they need. It helps to compensate to some extent for the problems of short-term memory. Many of us have had the experience of putting something down and then forgetting where we put it. The ordering and checking of those with AS is a way of avoiding this problem.

People with AS find change frightening. They know that adapting to change and solving new problems are things that they find hard. Consequently they tend to cling to their usual ways of doing things, even in the face of clear evidence that this is not working. When it becomes clear to them that they are faced with something that they cannot manage, it is not uncommon to find that people with AS can react quite catastrophically, having major tantrums, or even becoming violent.

> *Jane lived in a home with two other adults who had learning disabilities. Jane had AS and a mild learning disability, but she appeared much more able than the other two residents. She spoke fluently and well, and people were often deceived, thinking she was much more able than she actually was. A new member of staff joined the care team, and this new person liked Jane. She said to her one day, 'I think we should rearrange your room tomorrow. It is very untidy, and I am sure we could make it work better for you.' Jane did not really understand what she meant, but smiled and said, 'Yes.' The next day, Jane went to college in the morning. She came home to find that her new care worker had completely rearranged her bedroom and had (as she saw it) sorted out Jane's storage of her clothes into a much better system. Jane was deeply upset, and when the care worker left her to begin preparing lunch, Jane smashed up her room, throwing her clothes out of the window.*

Jane had not really processed and understood what the new care worker was proposing to do in her room, and the care worker clearly had little understanding of what it means to have Asperger syndrome. When faced with the sudden change in her environment, Jane could not deal with it, and her frustration and distress erupted in the destruction of her surroundings.

Because they have such difficulty with problem-solving and 'thinking on their feet', people with AS tend to react badly to change, and life at home will be calmer and easier to manage if unnecessary change can be avoided as much as possible. Redecoration of their surroundings, for example, can be very stressful to someone with AS. Moving house will be a huge challenge. Of course, many people find such changes difficult, but for those with AS they can be terrifying.

Managing change

If you know that someone with AS is going to have to cope with a change, then you can help them to cope better by means of some careful preparation. Think about how the impact might be minimized. If, for example, there has to be some redecoration or major cleaning work done in the home, then it may be wise to try to arrange for the person with AS to be somewhere else. A family visit or a short holiday may make the upheaval easier to manage. Don't forget, though, that going away from home, even for a positive reason such as a holiday, can still be stressful and anxiety-provoking. This may need quite a lot of advance planning and preparation to avoid any difficulties.

Discuss what is going to happen in advance with the person with AS, and explain in detail why the change is necessary. The timing of this discussion is tricky too. If you start talking about the change too far in advance, you are likely to provoke additional anxiety, and in some people this may result in lots of anxious questioning. If you leave it too long, they will not have time to get used to the idea before it all starts to happen. People will vary in what they can handle, so you may have to experiment to find what works for each person. Probably a week or two in advance of the change will be plenty for most people.

Where someone lives in a group home or other residential setting, one of the major causes of difficulty is that of changing staff. Inevitably staff members leave occasionally, and new ones arrive. In cases of sickness, there may be a need to use agency or other replacement staff. These kinds of changes can cause a great deal of anxiety for the person with AS, and they will often ask repeatedly for reassurance that their favourite staff members are coming on duty. They may also get very worried that new members of staff do not know their routines, and how to look after them properly. This may provoke a lot of questions, but it may also, in some cases, lead to a violent outburst. As a result, it is wise to handle such changes carefully, and take time to sit and explain to the person with AS what is going to happen. You will need to give them time to absorb the information and ask any questions that they have.

> *Roy has always found it difficult to cope with new people. It takes him a long time to get to know his care workers, and to trust them. Consequently, when there are changes of staff, he gets very anxious and agitated, and it takes him a long time to accept anyone new. Recently his favourite carer left the home where Roy lives, and a new person came to replace him. Roy became very agitated about this new person and eventually attacked him. When it was possible to calm him down and find out what had caused this, it came out that Roy thought the new person had stolen his favourite carer's job.*

This kind of difficulty is more likely to arise with someone whose level of ability is below average, although similar misunderstandings can arise with anyone with AS. It would probably have been possible to avert this attack if someone had felt able to sit down with Roy in advance of this change and discuss his worries. If this had been done by his favourite care worker before he left, then this would have been even better, because he could have made it clear to Roy why he was leaving.

Unfortunately, if someone gets a reputation for 'being difficult' and reacting badly to change, then people often become fearful of confronting them with information that they know will be upsetting. In fact, it is probably much better to do this in advance of the change, and leave plenty of time to deal with any anger or distress that may emerge. It does take skill and sensitivity to do this well, and while it may seem easier to avoid it, the outcome can be much worse if you don't tackle the problem head on.

If you are caring for someone with AS who you know can react badly to change, it is probably also wise to brief any new members of staff thoroughly about the person's likes and dislikes, and to make a point of introducing the person to any new staff members. This will enable the person with AS to find out a little about the new person in the presence of someone familiar. They will feel much safer in these circumstances than if someone new suddenly appears one morning, even if they know that a new person is coming.

It may also help to have a written summary of the person with AS in their notes, with any key issues highlighted, so that anyone new can quickly pick up the important information that they might need to know about that person. If the person with AS knows that such a summary exists, this can also reassure them that each newcomer will know the important things about them straight away.

The need for routine

The fear of change means that most people with AS love to have routines. They will develop routines and rituals around each part of their day, and left to themselves will happily work through them in their own time. They find this sameness very comforting and reassuring. Most of us do this to some extent. Think about your routine for getting up in the morning. It is probably fairly fixed, and if you have to change it because, say, you have run out of milk and can't have your usual coffee, or the boiler goes out and there is no hot water for a shower, you will feel put out and irritated. For people with AS this feeling is magnified considerably. In addition to irritation, they will often be very anxious. Change means unpredictability, and they do not know what might happen next. Moreover, they are not confident that they could cope with whatever it is.

Sometimes, the fact that they will move happily though their routines at their own pace can cause problems. Some people are so locked into their set pattern that it takes up a large part of the day, and they then fail to get to where they need to be.

> *Louis spent a long time every morning on his personal care. He had been brought up to believe that this was important, so he had developed a precise routine to follow every morning. He shaved, showered, washed his hair, dried himself, combed his hair, cleaned his teeth, and put on his clothes, in a slow, careful and meticulous manner. When he finally emerged, he would be immaculately dressed, without a hair out of place. Unfortunately, even though he got up at about eight o' clock every morning, it would take him until ten to be ready for breakfast. As he was supposed to be at college for nine-thirty, this was an ongoing problem.*

Louis's case illustrates that in some ways the tendency to like routine can be put to good effect. Unlike many people with AS, his personal hygiene was not a problem. He had learned early in life that this needed to be part of his daily routine and for him it always was. The difficulty was the slowness and thoroughness with which he carried out this routine. Attempts to hurry him along would simply make him angry and stubborn, and those who helped care for him were at a loss to know what to do.

Two approaches might help here. One would simply be to try to get Louis up earlier, so he has plenty of time for his routine without it getting too late for him to go to college. This might work, if he could be persuaded to set his alarm clock an hour earlier. The other, which would require more commitment from Louis, would be to devise a timetable with a set amount of time for each activity, so that he would have a time limit on each one. He would probably need a lot of help in the early stages to get this established. However, this approach can be particularly useful if someone is taking a long time because they find it difficult to organize their activities effectively.

Occasionally people like Louis may be described as obsessional or obsessive-compulsive. However, this kind of problem is not the result of a mental illness. Those who suffer from obsessive-compulsive disorder are driven by irrational fears, such as that someone will be harmed, or some disaster will happen, if they do not carry out their rituals. Even carrying out their rituals does not really banish their fears for more than a few minutes. Most people with AS, on the other hand, derive comfort from their rituals, and only become anxious if they cannot do them.

However, occasionally people with AS can, like anyone else, suffer from obsessive-compulsive disorder, and if you feel that the person you support becomes extremely and irrationally distressed if their routines are interrupted, it may be worth helping them to seek a mental health assessment. Such problems can be difficult to manage, but may be helped by psychological treatment, or sometimes by drugs which help them to manage their anxiety too.

Occasionally, especially in shared living situations, the routines and rituals of those with AS can become very irritating or annoying to others. The constant activity or noise that may accompany some of these activities can become very wearing. Some people may collect things such as coins or stamps, and get a great deal of pleasure from counting them or looking endlessly through albums. Sometimes people will pace up and down, or tap things. Some people may want to play the same piece of music over and over again. This kind of behaviour can become a real problem in a shared house, but will be difficult to change. It may be that a change of living situation will be the easier solution! However, sometimes harmony can be restored by coming to an agreement about when and where these things should be done, so that the person with AS can continue with their activities without disturbing anyone else.

Questions, questions!

Repetitive questioning can be very wearing for those who are on the receiving end of it, and it is important to realize that this is not done just to be annoying. People with AS may ask the same question over and over again, and this seems to serve a number of purposes:

- They may have forgotten the answer.

- They may want to test you to see if you are trustworthy and always give the same answer.

- They may be worried about what may happen and want reassurance it is not happening yet.

- They may be looking forward to something and worry it may not happen at all.

If you care for someone with AS, it may help you to cope with this if you can understand why it happens, and what purpose it is serving for the person. We have noted the problems that people with AS have in concentrating and remembering. Sometimes they can have a great deal of difficulty focusing on what you are saying, and may remember only parts of it, or indeed none of it. By asking you to repeat it several times, they will gradually absorb more and more information each time, until they can remember most or all of it.

For some adults with AS, the issue of trust is a big one. They may have had so many negative experiences with other people that it will take some time before they feel able to trust someone new. Asking the same question over and over again, and checking that you give the same answer each time, will reassure them that you are trustworthy and are giving them an honest reply.

Sometimes the questions will be driven by anxiety about whether something will happen or not. If the something is dreaded or feared, like a visit to the dentist, then the questions will be to seek reassurance that the event is not happening yet. If the event is something that the person is really looking forward to, then the questions may be aimed at reassurance that it will still happen, and that nothing has changed that might prevent it.

One way to check whether the person is actually having trouble remembering is to ask, 'What did I tell you last time?' If they can tell you correctly, then it is likely that the answer is serving one of the other purposes. By careful questioning you may be able to discover what the real cause of concern is and thus offer more effective reassurance. If none of these approaches seems to work, and everyone is becoming irritated by the questions, then you may have to put a limit on them, by saying something like, 'I have told you the answer several times already. I am not going to answer any more questions until… [after supper, after eight o'clock, or whatever seems appropriate].' In this case you will need to make sure that everyone involved in their care gives them the same answer.

The need for rules

Knowing what the rules are in any given situation can help avoid the stress of being faced with problems and changes. In addition to liking sameness, and disliking change, most people with AS like to have rules. They are keen to know which rules apply to which situation, and once they understand the rules they will usually stick by them. This tendency to like rules can be put to good use in the early years. If a child with AS is brought up with clear rules about personal hygiene and certain areas of social behaviour, these are much less likely to be a problem later. However, when the person has reached adulthood without an established set of rules in these areas of life, it may be much harder to get them to accept such rules later on.

Nevertheless, rules can be useful when working with people whose behaviour has been known to be difficult in the past. One of my colleagues worked with a young man who was known to have sexually assaulted a number of women, including those who were paid carers. She told him at the beginning of their sessions together that if he behaved that way with her, she would not see him again. She had no problem from him from then onwards. Of course, this assumes that he was getting something that he wanted and needed from his sessions with the psychologist, otherwise this would not have worked so well.

Many social situations can be made easier for someone with AS if they are given a few basic rules of polite behaviour in a given setting. For example, if a new friend is coming to visit the family, the person with AS might be advised that:

- it is polite to introduce yourself

- it is polite to say, 'Pleased to meet you'

- it is polite to offer a cup of tea or coffee, and perhaps a biscuit or cake

- it is polite to sit or stand and talk for a while with the new visitor

- if you wish to leave the room and do something else, it is polite to say, 'Excuse me'.

In addition, you might remind the person with AS that it is *not* polite to:

- talk all the time

- stare

- not look at the person when they are speaking to you

- interrupt.

Of course, this is a lot for the person to remember. It may be helpful to rehearse these things just before the visitor arrives. Even then, the person with AS may forget some things. One of the difficulties with social situations is that they are so variable. What is acceptable behaviour in one setting may not be in another. Different age groups and different social classes do things in different ways, as do different races and cultures. This can be very confusing for many people, not just those with AS. However, certain basic rules, like those above, do apply in many settings, and the best that you can do is probably to help the person with AS develop a small armoury of acceptable social skills. You can discuss with them the fact that these rules do change in some situations, but that if they stick to what they know, they will not go too far wrong.

Generalizing rules

The person with AS may get to grips with the idea of a few rules that operate in a given situation, but then problems arise because they are not able to judge whether their rules should be applied in a new setting or not. This can cause difficulties or embarrassment either way. For example, a young man may have been taught that it is polite to greet his female relatives with a kiss on the cheek. However, this may cause embarrassment if he does the same thing when a new neighbour calls. A child with AS may be told off for drawing on his bedroom wall, but then go and draw on another wall in the house, because he has only been told not to draw on the bedroom wall.

The basic problem here is the lack of judgement. Someone with AS, whether child or adult, may not be able to judge whether it is appropriate to apply the rule or not. The moral here is to be careful, and very specific, about what you teach. It is better to teach a rule that will always apply, whoever the other person is, than to assume that someone with AS will be able to judge when it applies and when it doesn't. Once again, this comes back to the difficulty of adapting to change. A universal rule of greeting might be to smile and say 'Pleased to meet you' to a new person when you meet. Shaking hands can appear over-formal in some situations, while a kiss or hug will probably not be appropriate unless the other person is a close friend or relative. Similarly, a phrase like 'Well I must be going now' is a safe and inoffensive way of ending most conversations, whoever is the recipient.

SUMMARY

o   Change is difficult for most people, but can be terrifying for someone with AS.

o   Difficulties with problem-solving and thinking of new ways to cope make change a particular problem for those with AS.

o   It may be possible to teach problem-solving skills. It can also help to rehearse potential problems and have a plan worked out for each, so the person with AS knows what to do.

o   Unexpected changes can lead to panic and even violence if badly managed. Change should ideally be planned, with time taken to explain to the person with AS what will happen.

o   Rules and rituals help the person with AS feel safe. When having to go into a new situation it can help to make the rules explicit, and perhaps practise beforehand what will happen.

o   It is better to teach a few rules that will fit in the majority of social situations, than to try to teach the person how to judge what is appropriate in each case.

Chapter 8

Coping with Anxiety and Other Emotions

Anxiety is a most uncomfortable emotion, and is probably one of the hardest to manage. We all suffer from anxiety at some time. Faced with an examination, such as a driving test, or if we need to go into hospital for an operation, we would be an unusual person indeed if we did not feel some anxiety.

Anxiety is part of what is known as the 'fight or flight' response and it has its roots in useful biological survival mechanisms. It is the 'flight' part of the system. Anger is the 'fight' part, and comes into play when we need to defend ourselves. If we were attacked by a tiger, we would feel anxious or scared, and we would need to run as fast as we could to get away. The hormones which give rise to anxiety increase breathing rate and divert blood to the large muscles of the limbs, ready to run away. The heart beats faster, to get the blood to the muscles more quickly, and unnecessary activities like digestion slow down, as blood is diverted away from the stomach and intestines. When there is real danger, anxiety works in our favour. It is protective.

In modern society there are few actual tigers, and few occasions when we really need to run away. What happens instead is that we get anxious about things like problems at work, paying our bills, or what our children are getting up to. In these situations, anxiety is not really a helpful response, because our body is preparing to run away from something that we have identified as a threat, even though running away from this kind of problem will not actually solve it. Consequently, the body gets ready for action, but no action follows. The changes that occur become a hindrance rather than a help. Constant anxiety can lead to symptoms like palpitations, as the heart gets ready for action that never happens, and ulcers, because the stomach is never given a peaceful time to digest food properly. Chronic anxiety is not a healthy state, and it can lead to a range of diseases or disorders if it remains unrelieved.

It seems very likely that some of us are born more prone to anxiety than others. It has been shown that some children are more prone to show anxiety than others from being a few weeks old. They react more strongly to changes in routine or environment, and become more easily distressed by such changes. The extent to which people are troubled by anxiety varies, but it seems that those with AS are born with a greater tendency to anxiety than most. It is one of the biggest problems faced by those with Asperger syndrome, and underlies many of their behavioural strategies such as rigid routines and repetitive questioning.

The purpose of routines and rituals

One of the most notable aspects of those with AS is their tendency to develop relatively rigid routines and rituals around their daily activities. Many of these will help the person to manage anxiety and feel in control. Routines and rituals can be calming and soothing, because they make life predictable. While these rituals and routines can be seen as a way of managing anxiety, they do not seem to be driven by irrational anxiety in the same way that obsessive-compulsive behaviours are. Rather, they are a way of ensuring that life remains the same.

For most people with AS, their development of routines is a way of compensating for their poor memory and lack of problem-solving and organizational skills. By establishing regular patterns and routines in their life, the person knows what is going to happen at each part of the day. Life becomes predictable, and thus less threatening. When life is predictable there are no unexpected problems to solve, so the challenges presented by each day are minimized.

If these routines and rituals are disrupted, or the person is prevented from carrying them out, they may become very agitated, anxious or even angry. The security of their cosy world will have suddenly been threatened. However, this behaviour is not driven by a fear of something bad happening, as with someone who has an obsessive-compulsive disorder. For someone with AS the routine can be summed up as something that is comforting and reassuring to do, which thus avoids any worry about future uncertainty. For someone with obsessive-compulsive disorder, the routine will be something that has to be done, even when they do not want to do it, because unless the action is carried out, disaster of some kind will follow. The difference is subtle, but important.

Most of us have our own ways of doing things, and our own systems for storing or displaying our belongings, and we resent these being changed or interfered with. People with AS are no different, although their attachment to such rituals may seem excessive, and their response to interference may be quite extreme.

Joan had a large dressing table on which she kept an array
of family photographs and her collection of cosmetics.
She had these arranged in groups which had a special

significance for her. She would have to check and arrange these belongings each morning before she came down to breakfast. One day, when she was out of her room, one of her sisters went into her room and moved them all around. She intended it as a joke. However, Joan's sister was very upset when she went into her own room later and found that Joan had ripped up several of her favourite dresses in retaliation.

This may appear to be an extreme response to a change in her surroundings, but nevertheless Joan's need for order and sameness are the main reasons for her reaction. Her routines are not driven by a need to prevent anything bad from happening, so this is not classic obsessive-compulsive behaviour. Rather, her patterns of behaviour could be seen to offer comfort. Joan's ritual checking of her belongings helps her to feel in control of her environment. It is comforting to reassure herself that all her belongings are still present and arranged as she likes them. Her sister's interference provokes anxiety, but also anger. Hence she retaliates by destroying her sister's possessions.

However, for some people with AS, the rituals and routines they develop are more worrying, and may be indicative of mental health problems.

Saul was meticulous in his self-care. He spent three hours each morning showering and getting ready for the day. His family were desperate to reduce this, because if they did not manage to get into the bathroom before him, they could not do so until lunch time. For those who had to go to school and work, this often meant they had to go without a shower and this caused repeated family arguments.

Saul also spent three-quarters of an hour brushing his teeth. He brushed them so long and so hard that the dentist said he was wearing the enamel away. However, when challenged, Saul said he could not wash any less, or clean his teeth any less, because he was worried that he would not get rid of all the bacteria, and would develop an infection. Sometimes his father would lose all patience and drag him out of the bathroom. At these times Saul would have a panic attack and often collapsed in a hysterical state.

While not typical of those with AS, this kind of problem does occur from time to time, and it would be fair to say that Saul's daily routines are becoming abnormal to the point of mental illness. Saul is convinced that he will develop an infection if he does not carefully wash each part of his body, and clean his teeth, for a considerable length of time. If he is prevented from doing this, he becomes panic-stricken. These routines are driven by something more than the need for comfort, and it does not seem that indulging in them is a positive experience. Saul might benefit from receiving some professional help to manage his anxiety around this issue. Psychological treatment might help, with or without medication.

Managing anxiety

Managing anxiety is not always easy. Sometimes there are very good and sensible reasons for feeling anxious (remember the tiger). Sometimes the anxiety will only be reduced by dealing with the issue that is worrying. For example, if a person is worried about the lock on their front door being inadequate to keep out intruders, then they will not feel able to relax until the lock is replaced, or perhaps a stout bolt is added to the door. If, on the other hand, they are worried about being made redundant, this is largely out of their control, so there is little that they can do. However, they may be able to reduce their anxiety by looking for another job. Sometimes anxiety is the result of unhelpful patterns of thinking or irrational fears. In this situation the person may need to work on changing the way they think about things in order to minimize the anxiety.

There are also occasions when it can be very helpful to share the worries with someone else. Another view of the situation may help the anxious person to see that they are worrying unnecessarily, or may help them to decide on something they can do to reduce their concerns. This kind of help might come from a good friend, or from a therapist. If the anxiety is affecting the person's everyday life and preventing them from doing what they want to do, then therapy may be the answer. A trained therapist will have a number of techniques to help manage anxiety, including the use of cognitive behavioural therapy and relaxation (see below).

Emotional and social support

People with AS need help to understand the rules of social situations, and support to help them to cope when faced with new ones. This might be by discussion, role-play, or by going with them into a new situation and prompting them, or showing them how to do the correct things. Using role-play can be an excellent way of reducing anxiety about a forthcoming situation. This might be a visit to hospital, an interview, or joining a new club. By rehearsing what could happen, the kinds of things to say, and what to do, the person's worries about this event can often be reduced greatly. A visit to the physical location beforehand can also help to make it seem less frightening.

In a work setting, one technique which has been used a lot in the USA is that of 'job coaches' who go along with the person with AS to the interview, and also stay with them during the first few weeks of a new job. The job coach helps the person with AS to become familiar with the situation, the people and the demands of the job, and then gradually withdraws as they settle down. With less able people the job coach may always remain in the background to troubleshoot any difficulties that arise. This kind of support is very important in reducing the person's overall level of anxiety in a new situation, and makes it much more likely that they will be able to learn the job and cope with the demands of those around them. It can make the difference between succeeding or failing in the work situation. Unfortunately it is rare in the UK.

Cognitive behavioural therapy

One of the most popular approaches used to help in managing anxiety amongst the general population is that of CBT (cognitive behavioural therapy). This involves the person who is anxious learning to monitor their thoughts and to challenge them by means of behavioural experiments. They will be encouraged to try things out, to see if their imagined fears have any basis in fact. While this approach has its limitations, it can be very powerful and successful for some people.

Unfortunately CBT may be less helpful for many people with AS. Some of the most able people may be able to make use of some of the principles, but many of those with AS will not have the required capability of monitoring and challenging their thoughts. If you recall their difficulty of holding information in the mind for any length of time, and of making decisions, it is easy to see that this may not be the best approach for those with AS. Therapists working in mental health services are most likely to see CBT as the first line of defence in dealing with chronic anxiety. As a result, they may attempt to use this approach to help someone with AS, and this is particularly likely if they have little experience of the condition. While this may help some people with AS, for others it will probably become yet another source of stress, because they will not be able to understand what is required of them.

Relaxation

One of the standard ways to help manage anxiety for many people is to teach them how to relax. This approach usually depends on learning how to relax each part of the body in turn. Often the technique is supported by the use of the recorded voice of a therapist, who guides the person through the sequence. In theory this technique might work for someone with AS too, but in practice it may not be ideal. We have seen that people with AS often have difficulty interpreting language, especially long or complicated sentences. It is likely, therefore, that a recorded voice could add to tension, rather than relieve it.

While the traditional approaches to relaxation may not always be the most suitable, the principle of teaching someone how to relax generally is likely to be a valuable one. It may be necessary, though, to develop a more creative and flexible approach which will suit each individual, rather than using a 'one size fits all' strategy.

Many people find listening to music relaxing, although tastes vary greatly. If you plan to use this as an aid to relaxation, it would be advisable to spend some time finding out which kinds of music appeal to the person that you are trying to help. Using a background of pleasant music to other tasks, such as housework or cooking, may help the person to be more relaxed during these activities. However, be careful that they are not distracted by the music to the extent that they forget what they are supposed to be doing.

Solitude is often relaxing for those on the autistic spectrum, and one of the most relaxing activities for someone with AS is likely to be a period of time spent on their favourite special interest or hobby, on their own. This is especially likely to be helpful if they have had a busy and demanding period just beforehand. If you become aware that the person with AS that you care for is becoming agitated, then it may be wise to suggest that they spend some time alone in this way. Such a move can often defuse what might otherwise become a difficult situation.

Physical activity can, paradoxically, be very relaxing. Think how good you feel after a good walk, or a pleasant swim. Outdoor activities like gardening can also be relaxing. Simple yoga can be very effective, as it is primarily physical rather than psychological. People with AS will often gain a great deal of benefit from a period of exercise of some kind, especially if this also can be spent alone. You may need to help them organize this, especially if it is something like going swimming at a public swimming pool. Make sure that this will be in a relatively quiet period. A swimming pool full of screaming youngsters and splashing teenagers is likely to be stressful, not relaxing. Working in a gym, at various machines, may also be good for some people, but again bear in mind that many modern gyms have constant loud music in the background which is far from relaxing.

Do not be tempted to suggest that someone with AS gets involved with team games. Team games are social situations with many complicated rules involved, and those with AS are likely to find them hugely stressful. Solitary activities, or those with a sympathetic partner, are much more likely to be successful. Be aware also of the problems with co-ordination that some people with AS have. Many sports involve good physical co-ordination, and will simply be beyond the person's abilities.

In order to find what kinds of activities work best, you may need to experiment. The person with AS is unlikely to be able to tell you what they find relaxing, so you will need to be observant, and keep a careful watch on how they react, both during the activity and afterwards. Any signs of agitation will suggest that this is not a good choice for this particular person, and it will probably be a good idea to abandon the activity as soon as possible.

If an adult with AS lives in a residential setting, with carers on hand to offer support, it is likely that there will be many more opportunities to manage their anxiety before it becomes a serious problem. Setting up a regular timetable of activities, which include some relaxing ones as well as the more challenging ones, is likely to give a good balance to the day. Whether or not you have got the balance right for any given person will only become apparent after a while. Staff who understand people with AS can be invaluable in defusing potentially difficult situations, but for this good training is essential.

Practical help

While a listening ear, referral for therapy, and finding ways to relax can all help to manage anxiety, it is also worth thinking about the person's life on a wider scale. It may be possible to organize their way of living so that potential anxieties are much reduced. Potential problems can then be 'nipped in the bud'. Much of the anxiety suffered by those with AS is caused by their inability to cope with the demands of everyday life, and ensuring that they have the right support can reduce this significantly.

Help on a regular basis with tasks which are likely to cause problems can make a huge difference to those with AS. Where people live in supported living settings with regular help from someone they trust, many difficulties can be avoided or reduced. What kind of help may be important? This will depend on the person, and their level of ability generally, but the following are likely areas where practical help may be needed:

- establishing a satisfactory daily routine for self-care and cleaning the home

- managing money and paying bills regularly

- regular help to manage the home, in areas of maintenance, safety, organization, etc.

- rapid access to someone trusted to help with unexpected problems

- help with shopping, planning meals and cooking.

It is not too difficult to imagine that if you felt unable to cope with any or all of the above, you might feel anxious for much of the time. Many people with AS do not receive this kind of help, both because they often seem too able in other ways to need it and because they do not think to ask for it. Many people with AS need this kind of support, but do not get it because there is no money available to fund it.

From anxiety to anger

Anxiety and anger are both parts of the same hormonal system. They are the opposite ends of the 'fight or flight' system discussed earlier. If you do not run away, you turn and fight. It is easy for anger to turn to fear (or anxiety), and for anxiety (or fear) to lead to anger. People with AS worry about everything, and as a result their tolerance for frustration is lower than usual, and they may be more easily provoked into anger. What might seem like small things to the rest of us can trigger a reaction from someone with AS which seems out of all proportion to what has happened.

Imagine for a moment that you are incredibly stressed, and that everything around you seems to be going wrong. You are desperately trying to hold your life together, and then someone comes along insisting that you do something for them right away. Imagine also that you do not fully understand what is being asked of you. Even though the something may be relatively trivial, it is possible that you would react with an angry outburst. A bystander might think that your response was out of all proportion to what had been requested, but they would not know how you were feeling inside. So it is often for those with AS. Unfortunately, as a result, they are often labelled as difficult, unpredictable and even dangerous. In fact, they are simply stretched to the limit in terms of their ability to cope. Much of this apparent explosiveness has its roots in anxiety.

Because of this link, it is important to try, as far as possible, to help someone with AS keep their anxiety within manageable bounds. It is doubtful that the person will be able to tell you when their anxiety levels are becoming unmanageable, but if you know someone well you can usually see when they are becoming more agitated, and you may be able to take action in one of the ways suggested above to reduce the anxiety levels. Taking action early on may avoid the escalation that leads to an angry outburst, or perhaps even violence.

Signs to be aware of

An early sign of agitation may be an increase in ritual or obsessional behaviour patterns. Someone may obsessively check their belongings or surroundings. They may ask the same question or questions over and over again. They may pace up and down restlessly. It is easy as a carer to get irritated and feel impatient when faced with these behaviours, but if you respond to them with irritation or anger you risk making the situation worse. Patient questioning on your part, or a willingness to listen, may help to defuse what could otherwise escalate into a real problem.

The next stage is likely to be more obvious agitation. The person may swear, shout, slam doors or hit walls. You ignore such signals at your peril. However, by the time someone is this upset, it is unlikely that talking to them at any length will help, unless you have a very good, trusting relationship with them, and are confident you can calm them down. Otherwise, you might find that encouraging them to go into a room on their own and listen to music, or spend some time on their favourite hobby or interest, may help them to calm down. Another approach might be to suggest that you go for a walk with them. The act of walking is likely to be calming, and as you walk you might gently enquire what the problem is, and see if they can tell you. In some residential settings, there may be opportunities to ride an exercise bike, or hit a punchbag, and these may also help to reduce the person's level of agitation.

If the situation has gone beyond this, and the person is already beginning to cause damage, then it is probably wiser to back off and let them work through their explosion. Obviously if someone is at risk of harm, then more decisive action will have to be taken, and you may even need to call the police. However, such an extreme reaction is less common. More typically the person will destroy or damage their own belongings or perhaps damage their immediate surroundings. While not ideal, this is less worrying than if other people are being put at risk.

If someone with AS has had an outburst of this kind, it is probably worth trying to explore the problem with them later, but you will need to be sure that they have calmed down before you do so. If you approach them too soon, you risk resurrecting their anger all over again. Once they are calm and you can explore the problem carefully, you are likely to find that the root of it is a misunderstanding. The person with AS is likely to have 'got the wrong end of the stick' and has reacted not to what really happened but to what they thought was happening. Sometimes the explosion will be the result of feeling overwhelmed by the demands of the situation. However, sometimes the person will react violently simply because they do not understand what is going on.

> *Carl attended college twice a week. He was a highly anxious person who constantly asked the lecturers and other students about what was going to happen next, and where he should be. Students were often told off if they did not get to the right place at the right time, and this added to Carl's worries. One day there was an unrehearsed fire drill. Carl was told that all the students had to go outside. He was very worried because he knew he had to be at his French class at that time. When he asked the lecturer why he had to go outside, he replied, 'Because I say so.' Carl kicked the lecturer hard on the shin, and as a result was later suspended. He felt very angry and resentful about this. Although Carl had behaved very badly, if the situation had been explained properly to him, then it is unlikely he would have reacted as he did.*

At other times, there may be a genuine grievance or concern that the person with AS has been trying to get resolved for some time, without success. They may have tried to communicate their concern, only to have been brushed off, or to have failed to make themselves understood. If this happens several times, their frustration may mount until finally they can hold it in no longer. It is not uncommon to find care staff who are impatient with people with AS, finding them irritating and tiresome. Usually this is because they do not understand the condition, and see the person as quite capable, but just being difficult. In such a situation, the staff are unlikely to listen or take an interest in much that the person with AS says. This can lead to these kinds of outbursts.

> *Anthony had irritable bowel syndrome and he often had to use the toilet at short notice. He moved into a new home where the toilet was in the bathroom. As a result, he often found himself desperate to use the toilet when someone else was in the bathroom. He complained to the care staff that he needed to have access to another toilet, or at least to have a commode in his room. The staff became irritated with Anthony. They did not believe that he could not wait to use the toilet. Later, when they found soiled newspaper in his room they became very angry with him. Anthony felt very angry and misunderstood, and that night he smashed up his bedroom.*

While this kind of behaviour is never acceptable, it is easy to see how someone may become extremely frustrated in a situation where either they fail to understand what is going on or they cannot make their own concerns understood to others.

Using anger and violence to control

Occasionally, as a result of a few experiences such as those above, some people with AS will learn that anger and violence are good ways to control others in their environment. They learn to use such behaviours as a way of getting others to leave them alone and stop making demands. This kind of pattern is both unhealthy and dangerous, and if you see signs of such a pattern developing, it would be a good idea to seek psychological help for the person concerned. You can usually do this via a referral from their family doctor. Often this kind of behaviour can be contained by firm, clear rules, and a refusal to be brow-beaten. However, the watchwords must be calmness and firmness. If you respond to such behaviour with anger or aggression, you are likely to be putting yourself, and possibly others, at risk. If you are at all concerned about someone's aggression and anger, then seek professional help.

Think Asperger

In helping those with AS to cope with their anxiety, it is helpful if you can begin to 'think Asperger'. Our modern society is incredibly noisy, complicated and demanding. If one lives in a busy town, there is rarely a time when it is truly quiet, except perhaps in the middle of the night. If you live in London, it is never quiet. Most of us learn to adapt to a constant level of noise and stimulation. Generally we do this by screening out much of what comes our way. We focus on what we want to see and hear, and ignore the rest.

People with AS find this extremely difficult to do. They often see, hear and feel everything to a much greater extent than most of us, and much of their energy is used up in coping with all this stimulation. Add to that the confusing and complicated social demands that come from other people, and you can see that life might quickly become overwhelming. If you find this hard to imagine, then see if you can borrow a video camera of some kind, or a mobile phone with a camera. The recording you make needs to have sound too. When you play your recording back, turn up the sound as far as you can. If you can watch the output on a large screen that will also help. What will probably surprise you is how much is going on, and how much noise there is. When you were in the real situation, your brain was filtering out a lot of this. However, for people with AS, their brains are much worse at this kind of filtering, and their experience will be much closer to your film.

Thus, when you are thinking about how someone with AS may cope in a new situation, think Asperger. Think about how many people there will be, and how many of these will expect the person with AS to interact with them. Think about the overall level of noise and other stimulation. A swimming pool, a large store, a party or a disco can present an overwhelming level of noise for someone with AS. Think also about other kinds of stimulation. Bright lights, strobe lights, excessive heat or cold, and so on can all be distressing to someone with AS. It is well known that children with autism react badly to such situations, but many people with AS, even as adults, find them difficult too.

Tony Attwood, in his book *The Complete Guide to Asperger's Syndrome*, describes how he 'talks Asperger' too. Although much of what he is saying relates to children, the principle that he advocates is a sound one for adults too. He describes talking in short, simple sentences, leaving time between each phrase for the person to take in what has been said, and digest it. This can also help to reduce anxiety, because the person with AS is not struggling to keep up and therefore worrying that they are missing the important part or forgetting something crucial.

Coping with other emotions

People with AS generally seem to express their emotions a little differently than most of us. The lack of facial expression has been noted in the diagnostic criteria, and this may make it difficult to decide how someone with AS is actually feeling.

As described above, there may be other non-verbal cues, such as pacing or hitting things when angry, but less extreme emotions may be harder to read. In addition, many people with AS have remarked on the difficulty they have in expressing their feelings in words.

Sadness and loss seem to be particularly difficult to express. Often it seems that such feelings are expressed in a form that looks more like anger. Occasionally people may latch on to a phrase which they think expresses their distress, but actually conveys something much more extreme. Someone may say 'I want to kill myself' or 'I want to die' when what they really mean is that they are upset about something. On the other hand, someone may be experiencing quite a powerful sense of loss, but not show any outward signs of it.

Some people with AS find music is helpful as a way of mediating and expressing their sadness, and may play a favourite piece over and over again if it gives them comfort. Others will want to talk about a loved person who has been lost, at every opportunity. Even though they may not cry, or show other obvious signs of mourning, this rehearsal of what has happened and how they miss the person seems to be their way of expressing what they feel. Unfortunately, other members of the family who are dealing with their own grief may find this difficult to handle. They may feel that the person with AS is being insensitive.

Understanding how people with AS deal with their emotions can help those around them to cope with their reactions more sympathetically. People who do not have AS show considerable variation in how they express emotions, so it is not surprising that those with AS do too. It is vital to remember that their differences in dealing with emotions are 'hard-wired'. That is, they are part of the way the person's brain is made, and will not change much with time. While some of the strategies that have been discussed above can help, these differences will not go away. To a large extent, the world will need to adapt to the person, rather than the other way around.

SUMMARY

o   Anxiety is uncomfortable and unpleasant, and people with AS are more anxious than most.

o   Rituals and routines often serve to help people with AS to control their environment and thereby manage their anxiety.

o   These rituals and routines seem to be comforting, rather than being driven by fear as in obsessive-compulsive disorder.

o   Standard approaches to teaching relaxation may be of limited use, but including restful and relaxing activities in the person's daily routine can help them to stay more relaxed.

o   A chance to talk about their worries with a sympathetic person can help a great deal. However, conventional therapy such as CBT may be less helpful to someone with AS because of their problems of attention, language and memory.

o   Practical help and a structured way of life can considerably reduce the tendency to anxiety.

o   Anxiety which gets out of control can lead to temper outbursts and even aggression.

o   A person with AS may sometimes learn to use anger to keep others away and to avoid demands. This needs to be discouraged as soon as it appears or it may lead to serious problems.

o People with AS find it difficult to talk about how they feel, and have trouble expressing other feelings such as sadness after a loss. Alternatively they may use words which express extreme emotions that are not really meant.

Chapter 9

Obsessional Interests and Other Common Characteristics

Obsessional interests

One of the defining characteristics of people with AS is their obsessive interest in one or more topics. These can vary enormously from an interest in the music of an obscure composer to being able to recite the names and locations of every television transmitter in the UK. Typically these special interests will centre around something which is outside the usual range of hobbies and interests, and the person with AS will often develop an extremely detailed knowledge of the subject.

Sometimes an obsession with a topic seems to arise out of a childhood fear, so that a fear of the noise of a washing machine may lead to a fascination with washing machines in general. At other times, a TV programme or a book may trigger an interest in something and the obsession grows from there.

Harry has an obsession with 'Star Wars'. He has seen all the films several times and has DVDs of all of them which he watches regularly. He knows all the characters and the details of the actors who played them. He can recite sections of the dialogue, especially those he finds funny. He will spend hours talking about 'Star Wars' to anyone who will listen, and he loves watching his DVDs.

While many people, especially children, may share these kinds of interests, what distinguishes the interests of the person with AS is the level of detail that they collect. If the interest is in soap operas, the person with AS may know the name of each character, the number of the house they live in, the name of the actor who plays that person, when they joined the programme and so on. If the interest is in trains, the person with AS will probably know every model made, where it was made, how many years it ran for, what routes it ran on, and how many were made.

The topics may change over the course of someone's life, or they may last for years. Some people will have more than one interest, and others will have only one. Typically the focus of the interest is in objects, or machines. The person will spend hours gathering information, reading books, watching videos, and possibly using the internet too. They can become experts on their particular topic or topics, and may sometimes be able to capitalize on their knowledge to obtain work. Some people may make a significant contribution to academic or practical knowledge as a result of their interest, producing new designs or new theories.

In young people and children, the interest may provide a route whereby other more basic skills can be developed. The youngster may be more willing to work on an essay about his or her favourite topic than on something which is of no interest at all. Skills such as spelling, grammar and the ability to write clearly can all be improved in this way. Some people with AS have achieved a high level of academic success by studying their special interest.

The special interest may also provide a way of making contact with others and developing friendships. An interest in model trains, for example, might lead to membership of a local group devoted to this interest. In such a setting, the person with AS may seem less odd, and his or her fund of knowledge may be welcomed by others. This can be a very positive means of overcoming some of the other social difficulties experienced by those with AS, and may give a boost to their self-esteem and sense of worth.

> Simon had a special interest in steam locomotives. He knew all the different types of locomotive, when they were made, who by, and the routes that they ran. Simon had few friends, and his aunt suggested that he joined the local model train enthusiasts club. Simon was worried about going there alone, but his cousin went with him the first few times, and soon Simon was happy to go alone. He became well known amongst the members for his detailed knowledge of steam locomotives, and other members would often seek him out to find out about a particular engine. Simon not only made friends but became something of a celebrity at the club.

At other times, however, the obsessional interest can become a hindrance. It may get in the way of the person carrying out essential routine activities such as washing, cleaning or cooking. It can also prove to be a social barrier because it is the only topic that the person with AS is interested in. In conversation, they may dominate, and even talk over others, in order to be able to talk about their interest. This will have the effect of driving people away, and given the difficulties that people with AS already have in socializing, this additional handicap is not helpful.

If this kind of behaviour is becoming a problem, it may help to try to put limits around the amount of time which you are willing to spend talking with the person about their special interest. Given that it is so enthralling and rewarding for the person with AS, it would perhaps be unkind to refuse to listen at all, but you might want to specify a time for the conversation to take place, or put a limit on how long it will last. You could agree, for example, that you will spend fifteen minutes at the end of each afternoon discussing their favourite topic. Sometimes you might use the promise of a period of time talking about, or taking part in, the interest as a reward for engaging in the more mundane but necessary activities.

As described above, the obsessional interest can result in people being alienated and bored by the person with AS. It is important to try to make the person aware that not everyone will share their fascination with the topic. Those with AS may benefit from being taught about other simple topics for conversations, such as the weather, TV programmes, sport, and so on, which they can use instead to engage with other people.

You might also try to help the person develop an awareness of when the person they are talking to is becoming bored. This would involve trying to help them notice if the other person is looking away, moving away or attempting to change the subject. Not everyone with AS will be able to learn and make use of such signals, but some may be able to. You will probably need to role-play this a number of times, as well as reminding the person with AS from time to time, but it can work for some people.

Types of special interests

You will not be in the company of a person with AS for long before they start to tell you about their special interest. These can include collecting things such as stamps or coins, an interest in particular types of machine, such as cars, trains, motorbikes, aeroplanes, tractors, etc., or an interest in a particular composer or scientist. Others become fascinated by astronomy, maths or physics. Sometimes it may be an interest in a particular type of TV programme or film. However, some people have special interests which at first sight are less obviously related to AS. It appears that these less obvious interests occur more often in women with AS, and might be, for example, an obsession with diet and food, which can sometimes be mistaken for an eating disorder, or an obsession with cleanliness and hygiene, which may look like obsessive-compulsive disorder. Indeed it is often very difficult to draw a clear line between these various conditions. If someone has such an obsession, it may be wise to suggest a professional assessment to try to clarify whether there is a real cause for concern.

> *Fiona had an obsession with her weight. She felt that she must never weigh more or less than nine stone. She weighed herself three times a day, and if her weight varied at all, she ate more or less accordingly. Fiona had a very restricted range of foods that she would eat, and could tell you exactly how many calories each portion of her food contained. However, she never became distressed about her weight, she simply changed the amount she ate in response to any change in her weight.*

At first sight, this might look like an eating disorder, but it is different in a number of ways from the classic patterns of anorexia or bulimia. Fiona does not get distressed about changes in her weight, she simply moderates her eating. She is not obsessed with being fat or thin, but has decided that her optimum weight is nine stone and sticks obsessively to that. She is not putting her health at risk by losing excessive amounts of weight, and she never makes herself vomit.

Women and girls also seem to be more likely to develop an obsessive interest around animals, or fictional characters such as those in books or soap operas. Sometimes they may become fascinated by a fantasy or fictional world as in books, films, games or on the internet. Of course boys and men may also have these kinds of interests.

> *Jo was obsessed with horses. Like many teenagers, she loved to ride, and her bedroom was full of pictures of horses. Jo knew all the different breeds and where they originated. She could tell you how tall each breed would grow, and what they were first bred for. In all these ways, she was not too different from some of her horsey friends. However, her mother began to worry when Jo expressed a wish to sleep in the stables with the horses.*

This kind of identification with animals is not uncommon in youngsters like Jo. Their interest in itself is not necessarily unusual, but they want to take it to extreme lengths. In cases like this it is important to put firm limits around such behaviour before it becomes established. Once these kinds of behaviour are established in an adult it will be much more difficult to change them.

When to worry

Sometimes the content of the special interest can be worrying. If someone has an interest in weapons, or how bombs are made, or in poisons or pornography, for example, other people may become very concerned, even if the person with AS shows no immediate inclination to put their knowledge into practice. In these kinds of situations, it may be prudent to try to modify the interest into a related but more socially acceptable area. An interest in weapons and bombs might be directed into an interest in the military generally, or even into war-gaming. An interest in poisons might be widened into a more general interest in how drugs work or in chemistry. Pornography will tend to be more difficult to change, but it may be possible to serve the person's sexual needs by explicit magazines which are on more general sale. Making these changes will not be easy, and will require a lot of tact. It will also require that you engage with the person about their special interest in some depth, at least for a while. You will need to introduce the new topic gradually as a slight variation on the existing interest. Perhaps the purchase of a new book where the new topic and the old overlap can be the beginning.

> *Edward was fascinated by machine guns. When he was quite small he was taken to an army show, and saw the soldiers practising with a machine gun. At the time he was terrified by the noise, but subsequently he became interested in how they worked, and began to collect information about all the different kinds. By the time he was twenty, he knew all about machine guns. He could tell you when the first ones were made and used, and which countries had which types. Edward's father was worried about his son's interest, but Edward never showed any interest in possessing or firing a machine gun. Indeed after that first time, he had never seen a real one. He did not even particularly like to see films of them as he still found the noise alarming.*

Although at first sight Edward's special interest might appear worrying, it is clear that his fascination began as a way of mastering his fear of the gun that he saw and heard. Over time it became an academic interest, and he had no interest in what the guns were used for, or in using one himself. While others might feel more comfortable if he did not have this interest, it is unlikely to cause any real problems. However, if his family wanted to divert his interest to less worrying areas, they might consider trying to interest him in other army equipment instead.

Generally speaking, the focus on a special interest and the time spent exploring it are positive aspects of life for most people with AS. We have already noted that spending time alone on one's area of special interest can be comforting and relaxing for some with AS. However, there are times when either the content or the amount of time spent on the activity becomes worrying. While it is difficult to be specific about when a particular area of interest should be a cause for concern, probably the best indicator is the person's emotional state. If, while engaged in their topic, they seem relaxed and content, then probably all is well. If they appear agitated or restless, or actually distressed, then it is possible that the interest is a less than healthy one. If you feel that their interest is leading them to harm themselves or others, then you should definitely seek professional advice.

Financial implications

Occasionally you may find that someone with AS is spending a huge amount of money on their interest. If, for example, they are interested in coins, stamps or old books, they may spend a lot of money on particular items that they want. This need not be a problem, as long as their bills are paid, and other basic needs met. However, such an interest, and the desire to add to a collection, may lead to exploitation by others. While this is a risk faced by anyone in this kind of situation, those with AS may be particularly vulnerable because they are generally less socially skilled, and are less likely to be aware of this risk. If you become aware that this may be happening, then you may need to try to warn the person about such transactions. In some cases you may even need to involve the police.

> *Richard was interested in old coins. His interest had begun when, as a child, he was taken to see a Roman excavation. The shop next to it sold Roman coins, and Richard was able to buy one with his pocket money. This led to a fascination with old coins, and by the time he was thirty Richard had thousands of coins. His collection was worth many hundreds of pounds. Unfortunately, Richard started visiting a little shop in London that sold coins for collectors, and the owner of the shop soon realized how easy it was to persuade Richard to buy more. Over a period of a year, he sold Richard many coins, some of which, it was found later, were stolen. Richard was visited by the police, and when his father investigated further, he discovered that all of Richard's savings had been spent in buying coins from this person.*

Overall, though, the special interests of those with AS can be seen as more positive than negative. People with AS who are amongst the most able may contribute a great deal to human understanding by their study and research. For those who are less able, the interest may serve to protect them from the more difficult aspects of life, by being a source of comfort and entertainment. When the normal human world seems so complicated and hard to understand, the person with AS can take refuge in their interest, and be in control of their own world for a while. Adults with AS often comment that the pleasure they gain from their special interest outweighs anything else in their life.

Clumsiness

Most people with AS have some problems with muscular co-ordination. Children with AS have long been noted to be clumsy and poorly co-ordinated. They may have trouble learning physical skills, and often get into trouble for breaking things and knocking things over. They may have problems with balance, and be slow in developing skills such as riding a bicycle. Recent research has suggested that babies who later go on to be diagnosed as having AS show abnormal patterns of movement and reflexes from very early in life.

Although less immediately obvious, adults with AS are often clumsy too. The poor co-ordination noted in childhood tends to continue, so that the person is more inclined to damage or break things accidentally. They may also be inclined to bump into things or trip up more often than most people. There is often a problem in co-ordinating upper and lower body movement which may lead to an odd gait, or awkward posture. Lax joints may add to this problem; the child may be 'double-jointed', resulting in difficulties controlling certain postures or hand positions as in writing. Some people with AS have a conscious awareness of this disconnection, and feel that their body does not do what they want it to. Not only do they look awkward, they feel it too.

For some people these physical problems are primarily with fine motor co-ordination which makes it difficult for them to write well. Many people with AS have poor writing, and will often report having been told off frequently at school about this. The current generation of children, who can use a keyboard and a computer, may suffer less with this problem. However, this problem of fine motor co-ordination may make a number of everyday activities more difficult for someone with AS, and those who are helping or supporting them need to be aware of such difficulties.

Some people with AS report problems of dizziness and poor balance. As children they may dislike strongly the kind of games where they are swung around, finding this far too disorientating. Some people report sensations of the ground appearing to move beneath their feet at times, which can be very unnerving. These kinds of difficulties may make a number of different types of sports and activities such as fairgrounds unappealing to those with AS.

Some people with AS have problems following a rhythm, as in clapping in time to music. Activities like catching or kicking a ball may also be particularly difficult. However, some adults with AS have achieved excellence in sports such as swimming, trampolining, golf, running and horse-riding, all of which are characterized by the fact that they can be done alone. There is no requirement to co-ordinate with anyone else, and it may be that as a result they can develop the necessary skills in their own way and in their own time.

While underlying weakness in co-ordination may remain, everyday functioning can often be improved significantly by exercises designed to improve muscle control. It may be possible to teach in a 'hands-on' way when trying to improve skills such as handwriting, but some people with AS will find the touch of another person too invasive. Adults are also less likely to accept this form of teaching than children. For those who have difficulty in riding a bike, an exercise bike may help the muscle co-ordination, although it will not, of course, improve the balance. It is possible to improve motor skills in those with AS, in the same way as one would do with anyone else. Repeated practice will often make a significant difference. It is important, however, that this practice is done voluntarily and in an atmosphere of calm support and encouragement, and equally important that those helping are realistic about the limits of what can be achieved.

These physical difficulties may well have led to years of teasing and ridicule, and so adults with AS may be very sensitive about their problems. Helping them to improve these areas of functioning will require a lot of tact and patience. It will be important to build a trusting relationship with the person with AS before attempting to intervene. It is to be hoped that with earlier diagnosis of AS and better training for teachers, the coming generation of children with AS will not have to suffer the humiliation and ridicule that past generations have suffered.

Sensory sensitivity

Many people are aware that children with autism are more sensitive than average to many forms of stimulation in the environment. What is perhaps less well recognized is that this can also be true for those with AS. They can be particularly sensitive to noise, touch, food (especially taste and texture), colours, lighting and smells. Curiously they tend to be less sensitive than most people to extremes of temperature and pain. However, this is a much neglected aspect of AS, and if you do not ask the person about their experiences they will probably not think to tell you spontaneously.

Many adults with AS say that such sensitivities present more difficulties for them than managing emotions, making friends or finding a job. They report that many situations of daily life present them with sensory overload, which makes it even more difficult to function effectively. Indeed it seems likely that this contributes to the problems of concentration so often reported. The person is unable to screen out unwanted stimulation from a variety of sources, and thus it becomes impossible to focus on any one aspect of the environment and ignore the rest, as one needs to do in order to concentrate effectively.

Some people report a fluctuating sensory experience, especially when others are talking to them. The sound of the other person's voice can seem to vary from very quiet to very loud, as with someone turning the volume control of a radio up and down randomly. This means that they will often miss parts of what is said to them or what is going on around them. In order to fully understand what someone has said to them, they may need to have it repeated several times. Sadly not everyone is patient enough to do this.

People with AS can be particularly disturbed by sudden unexpected noises, high-pitched continuous noise, and confusing, complex or multiple sounds. Children can be particularly disturbing to some people with AS because they tend to emit all three kinds! Children with AS often find the noise, colour and bustle of the average school extremely distressing. The resultant sensory overload makes it impossible for them to focus on what is being asked of them. Active social situations like busy shopping centres, parties or sports centres can also be overwhelming for children and adults with AS.

Sensitivity to touch may take the form of a dislike of being touched by others, or a dislike of certain textures, as in clothing or bedding. Many children report disliking being hugged or kissed by relatives, and some adults find sexual touch unpleasant. Some people with AS even dislike having their hair combed or cut. This can cause particular problems in childhood, but these sensitivities also often persist into adulthood, and may be expressed in a variety of ways, including a dislike of new clothes and a tendency to keep wearing the same things. Other sensitivities may be unpleasant in the way that fingernails scratched on a blackboard are unpleasant to many people. Common dislikes are polystyrene, plastics of various kinds, and felt-tip pens on paper.

Food sensitivities may lead to the person being called a 'fussy eater', or in extreme cases may be seen as an eating disorder. While it is quite possible that someone with AS can also have an eating disorder, the problems are more often centred around dislikes of certain textures, tastes or even colours. These reactions can be intense, sometimes even leading to nausea. In general, food problems tend to decrease with age, but in an adult who has never been diagnosed, it is possible that unusual eating habits may have developed and gone unchallenged for years. In this situation it will be extremely difficult to change this behaviour in later life, even if this is desirable. Generally it will be easier to accept that the person cannot change these sensitivities and work around them as far as is possible to ensure that they still have a healthy diet.

Visual sensitivity can manifest in dislike of certain colours or colour combinations, or simply a dislike of bright lights. For some people these can trigger feelings of anxiety or even panic. These dislikes of certain colours mean that some people with AS will always tend to choose the same colour for their clothes, and some will actually refuse to wear anything which is not their favourite colour.

Maisie is an elderly lady who was only recently diagnosed with AS. She has lived in residential homes ever since her mother died and she was unable to cope alone. She initially received a diagnosis of schizophrenia, and has always been considered odd and eccentric by those around her. Maisie will only wear black. This began when her mother died and she was told that one should wear black while in mourning for someone. Maisie had never liked bright colours, and she came to love her black clothes. Now she will not wear anything that is not black. If she is given something of a different colour she will throw it in the bin, or give it away.

Other people with AS may have a particular dislike of one colour, perceiving it as too intense, and will avoid it at all costs. Very bright lights, as in shopping centres, supermarkets and so on, can also be very distressing to some people with AS. Such places can be very difficult to tolerate, because they combine many of the things that people with AS find most difficult: noise, light, bright colours, lots of people, and social demands. Remember that those with AS have difficulty screening out unwanted stimulation, and can become completely overwhelmed.

Sensitivity to smell may be less obvious, but in discussion with people with AS they often report some smells to be so strong as to be overpowering. The scents included in some soap powders may be so strong that they make the person with AS reluctant to wash their clothes or change them. It is worth exploring the issue of smells and scents, as this may explain a number of apparently incomprehensible behaviours. The perfumery department in a large store, for example, may be so overpowering that the person will run out of the store.

> Ian enjoyed going shopping although he preferred to go during the week when it was less busy. He would usually go with his sister, and they often went to have a cup of coffee and a cake while they were out. Ian's sister usually took him to a little tea-shop on the edge of town because it was not too busy and noisy. Unfortunately this shop closed down, and so, on the occasion of their last trip out, she decided to take him to the restaurant in the top of a large department store. To get to the restaurant, they had to go through the perfumery department on the ground floor. To Ian's sister's amazement and consternation, they had no sooner got through the doors of the store to go towards the escalator, than Ian turned round and fled out of the store. He could not bear the smell of the perfumes.

In contrast to the over-sensitivity to the above sources of stimulation, people with AS often show curiously little reaction to cold or pain. Similarly, excessive heat may not trouble some people, although some do report it as being unpleasant. A lack of response to pain can be particularly worrying because quite serious illness or injury may go unreported simply because the person with AS does not see it as a problem.

> *Douglas sprained his ankle while at work. He took the bus home as usual, and walked the half a mile from the bus stop to home, without any obvious problem. When he got home, he did not mention to his parents that he had hurt his ankle. When he came into the sitting room to watch TV later that evening, Douglas's mother was horrified to see his ankle was badly swollen. However, Douglas gave no indication of being in pain, and did not even limp. When his mother expressed her concern he seemed surprised.*

Managing sensory sensitivity

For some of these problems, avoidance is often the only effective strategy. However, with some people it is possible to gradually increase their tolerance by graded exposure to increasing levels of stimulation. Where excessive sound is troublesome, listening to music can often help to camouflage the noise, and wearing a personal stereo of some kind can help. An alternative and simpler solution is to provide the person with AS with earplugs. Plan necessary outings, such as shopping, visiting the doctor and so on for times when it will be less busy and noisy, and avoid large shopping centres and supermarkets.

Where you want to be certain that the person with AS will be able to hear and process what you are saying, avoid situations where there is a lot of background noise, and especially other people talking. Even then, because of possible fluctuations in their perception of sound, and their difficulties with attention generally, you may need to repeat yourself several times.

Sensitivity to touch may be helped by the use of massage or vibration. However, this is a difficult area, especially for adults, and it may be wiser just to respect their dislike of touch. This can cause particular difficulties in the area of sexual contact, where gestures of affection and caresses intended to be pleasant are simply intolerable for the person with AS. For a partner who does not have AS, and does not understand the problem, this can be hurtful and lead to resentment.

Where the issues centre around clothing, look at the sections on self-care and clothing in Chapter 4. Try different washing powders, liquids and softeners, and explore different types of fabric for clothing and bedding with the person with AS. Think about sensitivity to smell and texture. They may not think to tell you what the problem is unless you ask directly. When buying new clothes, try to ensure they are as similar as possible, in texture, fabric and colour, to existing and accepted clothes.

Food sensitivity is again a difficult area for adults. By the time someone reaches adulthood, they are likely to be fairly set in what they like and do not like. If their diet is really restricted, and you feel that their health is at risk, then it may help to do a little health education with them, around healthy eating and what we need to eat each day. A referral to a dietician may also help. It might then be possible to reach a compromise which will improve their diet, without causing undue stress. Be prepared to compromise and to be creative. Putting food through a blender to make a thick soup may solve a texture problem, or mixing the disliked food with a stronger flavour such as curry may overcome the dislike of a certain flavour. If the issue is around colour of food, then try to find forms of each essential food which come close to the favoured colours. It may, however, not be realistic to try to change the behaviour of an adult very much, however eccentric their choices may be.

Sensitivity to light or colour can often be managed by careful planning of outings and visits. Where strong light cannot be avoided, the use of sunglasses or a sun visor can help. If there is a dislike of a certain colour or colours, it is unlikely that this will change in an adult, and both you and they will have to work around it.

Pain and cold are two sensations which most of us avoid instinctively. If you feel that the person with AS that you care for seems not to notice these sensations, it may be worth spending a little time explaining the risks of ignoring them. Try to encourage the person to approach someone they trust to report pain, even if they do not feel that it is a major problem for them. If you are a regular carer for someone with AS, it may be worth asking them routinely whether they have any pain or discomfort of any kind. In the case of cold, it might be wise to arrange for their heating to operate from a thermostat, set at a safe temperature, so that they do not have to think about keeping themselves warm or cool.

Mixing of the senses

There is a rare condition known as synaesthesia, where the messages from the senses appear to get confused. Colours can evoke a taste, or a sound will produce a sensation of colour, for example. This is not specific to AS, but has been reported by a number of people diagnosed with AS. It is a condition about which relatively little is known. Once again, it may not be spontaneously reported because the person may not realize that this does not happen to everyone. It cannot be cured, but it may help to understand what otherwise may seem like very odd reactions to certain stimuli.

Antisocial or criminal behaviour

In Hans Asperger's original studies of AS, he initially felt that the condition included an antisocial or aggressive tendency. However, subsequent research has not borne this out. People with AS are statistically no more likely to become offenders or behave antisocially than any other group in the general population. When they do offend, this is often because they fail to realize that they are breaking the law, and have not appreciated how their behaviour will be seen by others. Sometimes aggressive or violent behaviour is simply a complete loss of control, because the person has become so anxious or distressed that they can no longer cope.

We have noted already that some young men with AS may behave in sexually inappropriate ways that can cause alarm. However, these episodes usually arise from an inability to understand what is appropriate behaviour and what is not. Often people with AS have a strong sense of right and wrong, and once they understand the rules they are likely to stick to them more rigidly than most people.

Occasionally, people with AS may behave antisocially or aggressively in response to a real or imagined injustice from someone else. We have seen how they may miss, or misinterpret, social signals, and this can lead to retaliation which is outside the acceptable bounds of society. One of the more striking aspects of people with AS is their capacity for long-term memory of details, and this often applies to others' actions which have hurt or upset them. They can nurse grievances for years, recalling every detail of the real or imagined harm that was done to them. This can result in retaliatory attacks years later. Often, however, the person will give ample warning of this to anyone who will listen, and it can be possible to defuse this behavioural time bomb by talking the event through with them several times, and exploring any possible alternative explanations of the other person's actions.

The other type of behaviour which can appear alarming is when the person with AS becomes obsessed by another person, rather than a particular area of interest. Often this will be someone well known from TV or films. For the person who is on the receiving end of this obsessive interest, it can feel as if they are being stalked. It is important not to encourage such obsessive interests in individuals, and, if this seems to be developing, to give the person with AS very clear rules about what is and is not allowed in terms of their own behaviour.

Generally, however, most people with AS are law-abiding, if slightly odd and eccentric, people. One of the most important parts of their support and education is to make sure that they understand the social rules that govern sexual and aggressive behaviour, so that they do not get into trouble with the law. Once someone has developed unacceptable behaviours in these areas, they can be very difficult to change. If the person that you support is having difficulties with their behaviour in either of these areas, then you should encourage them to seek professional help.

SUMMARY

o Special interests are characteristic of those with AS and can take many forms.

o Women may show slightly different patterns of special interests than men.

o Special interests are usually helpful and provide an escape for the person with AS. However, if these interests lead to distress, the person may need professional help.

o The content of the special interest may be worrying, but the interest is rarely translated into antisocial behaviour.

o Clumsiness is common amongst those with AS. They may have a number of problems with muscular co-ordination and these will have been apparent since very early childhood.

o There may be problems of fine motor co-ordination, most often noted in difficulties with handwriting.

o Sensory sensitivities can take a variety of forms, and can cause a great deal of difficulty. Different types of sensitivity call for different approaches, but some will only be helped by avoiding situations where the sensitivity is a problem. An awareness of these problems can explain some apparently irrational behaviour. Ask the person with AS about this area, as they will probably not think to tell you.

o Those with AS may not notice or report pain, but should be encouraged to do so, with an explanation of the risks of ignoring such symptoms.

o People with AS can be violent and antisocial, but there is no real evidence that they are more inclined to these behaviours than anyone else. Often their so-called anti-social behaviour arises as a result of not understanding social rules.

Chapter 10

Needs and Service Development

People with AS have a number of strengths, and the more fortunate amongst them are able to capitalize on these. Special interests, combined with a desire for order and perfection, can enable some people with AS to develop a successful career where such attributes are of value. They often have an exceptional eye and memory for detail which can be invaluable in some settings. For the most able people with AS, an academic career can offer the perfect setting, especially if they are able to pursue their interests alone.

Unfortunately, the majority of people with AS are not so lucky, and their social and other difficulties often hamper their progress in life. Many of them need help to cope with the basic activities of everyday life, and for those who also have a mild learning disability, life can be even more of a struggle.

Where the person with AS has never received a diagnosis, they are often at a greater disadvantage because neither they nor their families have any explanation or understanding of the reasons for their difficulties. Thus a good diagnostic service is one of the first and most important services that is needed. This needs to be easily accessed, ideally through the family doctor as a first port of call.

Diagnosis and information about AS

Despite the poor services that are currently available for those with AS, receiving a diagnosis can be hugely important, especially to an adult who may have struggled for years, feeling that they were the odd one out. Suddenly the diagnosis, together with an explanation of what that means in terms of actual difficulties identified, can put everything into place, and help the person and his or her family to make sense of what has been happening for years.

People with AS should be encouraged to obtain as much information as they can about the condition. When the diagnosis is made, the professional concerned should take time to explain carefully to the person, and their carers or family, what AS means and how it shows itself. It is important to be positive about what can be done, as well as honest about what cannot. There is no cure, for example, but the first question many people ask is: 'What can be done about it?'

There have been several very well-written biographies of people with AS which can be enormously helpful both to those who have the condition and those who are trying to help them. There are also a great many books available for children with AS, although fewer for adults. With the growth of the internet, there is a lot of information now available online, and usefully there are a number of sites where those with AS can communicate with others who also have the condition, and share experiences. Many people with AS have never met anyone else with the diagnosis, and it can be very helpful and reassuring to realize that they are not alone.

Most people who know someone with Asperger syndrome are aware that services are inadequate. Families are often dismayed when, having received a diagnosis, they ask what help is available. The answer in most parts of the UK is usually 'not much'.

If the person with AS also has a learning disability, it is usually easier to get some support for them. They will be eligible for funding for supported living and residential homes, and often for help in getting and keeping a job. If the person is of normal ability, however, none of this will apply. Whatever help they may get from health services will usually be provided through mental health services, even though Asperger syndrome is not a mental illness in the normal sense. Mental health services, however, will rarely have the expertise to support those with AS, although in some areas this is changing.

Needs of those with AS

So what help do most people with AS need? The list below covers the areas that have been identified by families, carers and the people themselves, in several different studies of what services are needed:

- social skills training and help in learning the rules of social situations

- advice and support to go out and meet others in a safe setting

- help to learn the necessary skills to get and keep a job

- advice and support in budgeting and managing money

- practical help and support with activities such as cooking, shopping and cleaning

- supported living opportunities which will give both independence and back-up.

Let us look at each of these areas in turn.

Social skills training and help in learning the rules of social situations

Social skills training for children and adolescents with AS is now relatively common. However, for those who have become adults without the benefit of a diagnosis or the opportunities for such training, social situations remain a minefield of potential difficulties.

Working in groups with other people with AS can be enormously helpful and reassuring. Apart from anything else it is hugely reassuring to discover that you are not the only person with such difficulties. While not naturally inclined to group situations, belonging to a group of people with AS can be a very positive experience for all its members, because perhaps for the first time ever they will be with a group of people who know what it is like to have AS. The group situation also provides a safe environment to practise new skills without embarrassment or ridicule.

Social skills training is not a panacea, and some people with AS will find it extraordinarily difficult to transfer what they have learned in the group to the real world. However, at the very least, it offers a safe and supportive forum to discuss their difficulties and to learn what are the most important social rules, such as those which relate to touch and sexual behaviour. Where adolescents have been able to receive such training, their difficulties are often much reduced.

Advice and support to go out and meet others in a safe setting

We have seen that one of the difficulties that many people with AS experience is that of being bullied and exploited by others. Frequent experiences of this kind while growing up can make adults with AS almost phobic about meeting new people, even though they often wish for friends or partners. It can be very helpful to have guidance about what does and does not constitute a good friend, and in deciding where might be good places to go and meet new people who are likely to be a source of real rather than exploitative friendship. In the early stages of this process, having someone who is willing to go along with them and smooth the path can also be very reassuring. Help can also be given to enable the person with AS to choose safer and more suitable places to go and make contact with others.

Some projects have tried setting up specialist social clubs or dating agencies for those with AS and these can be very helpful. However, what has been found, perhaps unsurprisingly, is that those with AS need help to set up and maintain these services. Without outside help, they are not able to keep things going for themselves.

Help to learn the necessary skills to get and keep a job

Getting a job requires a range of skills which many people find a challenge. For those with AS it can seem an impossible task. They need to have the skills to search effectively, to be able to decide if the job is suited to their abilities, to fill in an application form, to attend an interview and perform satisfactorily, and to provide suitable references. However, having completed all of these, and assuming that they succeed in getting the job, they have then got to be able to organize themselves to get there on time, suitably dressed, and then be able to cope with a whole range of new people, new tasks and new places. For many people with AS this array of demands is too much. Even where they are successful in getting the job, they may not be able to keep it. Jobs place a range of demands on people, including the need to be sociable, reliable, organized and punctual. As we have seen, people with AS find many of these difficult.

Job coaching, which has already been mentioned, began in the USA, and has been very successful in helping people with AS overcome some of these problems. The role of the job coach is to help in the finding of a job and the application process, and then, once the person starts work, to go along with them and help them to get to grips with the job, the people and the place. Once the person with AS becomes familiar with the requirements of the job and its environment, the job coach will withdraw, and may only visit occasionally after a while. The job coach also acts as a sort of ambassador between the employer and the person with AS, in case of problems.

For those with AS who are less able, the job coach may not be able to withdraw in the same way, and may have to maintain regular contact with the employer, troubleshooting any problems as they arise. As with other aspects of life for those with AS, misunderstandings on both sides often lead to unnecessary difficulties. The job coach, as someone who understands AS, can act as an interpreter between the two parties and will often be able to defuse what might otherwise escalate into a destructive situation.

It would be very helpful for many people with AS if such a service was widely available in the UK also. At present there is very little help available. Most of what is accessible is via mental health services and, as we have already seen, the staff in such services are much less likely to have an understanding of the kinds of problems faced by those with AS.

Advice and support in budgeting and managing money

Even for those who are most able, managing money can be a problem. The cognitive difficulties which are characteristic of AS make the planning and organization of such an activity much more challenging than it is for most people. This can be a difficult area, because sometimes the person with AS, quite understandably, will be highly suspicious of other people interfering with their finances.

At present there is almost no help available in this area, except what is provided informally by families and carers. Social services staff in the UK are explicit in their refusal to deal with such matters, and although organizations such as the Citizens Advice Bureau (CAB) can be very helpful with matters like this, it is unlikely that they would have the necessary understanding of AS to be able to help effectively. Help in this area needs to be built into whatever services are developed for people with AS, in the same way that the CAB provides help for the average person on the street if required. Maybe there could be specially trained advisors within the CAB service.

Currently it is possible for families or others to get legal help in managing the affairs of someone with AS, but in order to do so the person with AS would have to be assessed as being incapable of managing their affairs, and most people with AS, despite their difficulties, are not so impaired that they could be described as legally incapable in this area.

Practical help and support with activities such as cooking, shopping and cleaning

For all the reasons already outlined in previous chapters, many people with AS need help in these areas of everyday life. Frequently, it is not the skills that they lack, but the organizational ability. A great deal can be achieved by setting up plans and timetables which the person can follow. These can be pictorial or written. As already noted, people with AS usually find it easier to absorb diagrams and pictures than they do written instructions. Moreover, their love of routine and ritual can mean that if you can establish a regular routine of tasks into their daily life, they are likely to follow this reliably and these areas become much less problematical.

Where the person with AS has reached adulthood without such routines, it may be harder to establish them, but if they are aware of problems and asking for help, this may be an ideal moment to try to set up helpful rather than unhelpful routines. Often, the person's family have spent many years puzzling about why the person with AS is failing to do what seems obvious. Once there is an understanding of the nature of the difficulties, this can open the way to some creative problem-solving by everyone involved.

Supported living opportunities which will give both independence and back-up

For people with learning disabilities, or those with chronic mental health problems, residential placements and supported living are well-established options for living an adult life but with help on hand when needed. Both of these systems have their supporters and their opponents, and both have their strengths and weaknesses. Nevertheless, for many people who are eligible for such support, they provide a useful and neces-sary service. Currently, those who have a diagnosis of both AS and a mild learning disability get the best of what is available for people with AS, because they may be able to access such services. However, the downside is that the people they share their living space with may be very different from themselves both in levels of ability and actual needs. Furthermore, the staff who work in these services may be unfamiliar with AS and the needs of those with the condition.

Most people with AS, despite often expressing a wish for friends or partners, are happier on their own for much of the time. As a result, living in a large 'group home', such as those often provided for people with learning disabilities, is far from ideal. They will often find the levels of noise, activity and social interaction excessive, and this can lead to conflict. Similarly, living with people with mental health problems can cause different conflicts. People with mental health problems, because of their own stresses and difficulties, will often find it hard to tolerate some of the eccentric behaviours of those with AS. Similarly, people with AS are unlikely to be sympathetic to the feelings of their fellow housemates with mental health worries.

Staffing of such homes can also pose problems for someone with AS. Staff tend to move on and change quite rapidly and, as we have seen, people with AS find such change difficult. The rapid turnover of staff also makes it difficult to provide adequate training for the staff group, so they are rarely able to understand and effectively manage the difficulties of a client with AS, who will probably be the only one with AS in the home.

We have also noted the risk that those with AS will be bullied or victimized, and some people with mental health problems will be prone to such behaviour, particularly those who have a degree of personality disorder. Conversely, if the person with AS has difficulty in managing their sexual needs and behaviour, there is a risk they may victimize a fellow resident who has learning disabilities or is vulnerable in other ways.

It is apparent, therefore, that although such residential settings can offer a great deal of support in some ways, and may appear to be an improvement on the person's present situation, the current type of provision is far from ideal. Most people with AS would benefit most from the 'supported living' model which is now proposed in many areas of the UK for people with learning disabilities. The basic idea is that the person has a flat or small house which is their own (usually rented as a council tenant) and then they are provided with a number of hours per week of practical support from someone who comes to their home. This person may help with cleaning, cooking, shopping and so on. This has the advantage that the person with AS would have a considerable degree of independence, but would have support when needed. Good staff training would be needed, however.

This model has been strongly advocated in learning disability services, where it suits the most able group reasonably well. For people with AS, the disadvantages are likely to be that if they encounter a situation which they cannot manage, they may have nobody immediately available to help, or if they resent other people helping as 'interference' there are likely to be problems. It is also unlikely to work well if the person with AS is expected to be able to manage their own budget and pay their support staff. The other big problem area, certainly in terms of existing services, is the lack of training of the support staff in the understanding of AS.

The services that seem to work best are those which have been set up by specialist organizations, such as the National Autistic Society in the UK, where those who run the services and staff them are well trained and understand the problems faced by those with AS. These services, however, also tend to favour those who are less able, and there remains the problem of funding.

The current situation

At present, there are far too few specialist services for people with AS. Most adults with AS are in one of two situations: either they are still living at home with ageing parents or they are living alone and failing to cope. The latter case will often have arisen because the person with AS was living with elderly parents but they have died. The person with AS remains in the family home, and struggles on alone. If they are fortunate, they will have brothers, sisters or other relatives who take an interest and may offer intermittent support. If not, their plight will only become apparent when there is a crisis of some kind.

Many elderly parents are very worried about the future for their adult child with AS. Even where there has not been a formal diagnosis, they are usually aware that the person will not cope well on their own. Often, they will seek help from social services, but this will not be forthcoming because the person is not in acute need or distress. Services will not be willing or able to provide help until the crisis happens. This seems a very unsatisfactory and somewhat unethical way to proceed, but it is driven by the lack of resources available to social services.

Currently in the UK, people with AS fall neatly between the two stools of mental health services and learning disability services. Their problems are different from either group. Their needs are probably closer to those with brain injury or other neuropsychological difficulties, who are also a hugely under-resourced group. Over the past fifteen years or so, there have been many studies and projects across the UK looking at the needs of those with AS. Most of these projects have been funded by short-term money, in the form of research funds. Many have identified similar problems, and similar areas of need. Some have set up useful and valued support services and networks but, once the funding has run out, there has been no willingness by the authorities to provide long-term funding. This pattern has been repeated several times, but still there is little change.

One of the reasons for this inertia has been the fact that the numbers of adults identified with AS has been, and still is, relatively low. However, now that the condition is better recognized and understood, the rates of diagnosis in children are rising significantly. Educational services are slowly getting to grips with the needs of these children, but when they leave school their families are horrified to find that there is nothing waiting for them to move on to. Families have to struggle on alone, with support from specialist charities and occasional professionals who develop a particular interest in the topic of AS. As the numbers of these youngsters increase, there is likely to be increasing and more vociferous campaigning by them and their families for government to provide the kinds of support services needed.

What would help?

From the discussion above, it is clear that adults with AS have a range of needs which current services do not meet. At present, most people with AS are supported by parents, partners or siblings. While many of these people do a magnificent job, it is obvious that this kind of support may not continue indefinitely. Parents may become ill or die, partners become demoralized and leave, and siblings marry and have their own children, and need to give their time to them. Some people with AS actively resist help from their families, even where the family members are willing to give it. There is an urgent need to plan the provision of an integrated diagnostic and support service geared specifically to the needs of those with AS. This service would need several elements which would ideally be co-ordinated from a single point:

- a detailed and thorough diagnostic service for children and adults accessed via the family doctor

- an educational service which could train and support teachers and classroom assistants

- links with higher educational establishments to support adult students and train staff

- job coaches to help people into work, and to help keep them in work

- social skills and sex education training groups for children, adolescents and adults

- a practical, specialist support service that would provide personal and domestic help to adults living independently

- a specialist financial service to advise on money management and offer practical help

- specialist residential and supported living services with trained support staff

- adequate funding for all of the above.

This might seem like 'pie in the sky' to many. However, if you were to balance against the likely cost of such a specialist set of services the costs of all the current difficulties that arise from trying to fit people with AS into services that do not suit them, and of picking up the pieces when things go wrong, then this may begin to look more realistic. It would be interesting to know how many referrals to mental health services, admissions to hospital, and appearances in court might be avoided by the existence of such services. Add to this the distress, disruption and pain caused to those with AS and those around them by the current unsatisfactory provision, and it may not seem such an unreasonable path to follow.

Ideally there would probably need to be several levels of service, to cater for those from the lowest levels of ability to the highest. Some people might be better served by residential placements than by supported living for example. For the most able group, many of their needs might be met by the existence of suitably trained helpers or counsellors who might be on call when needed, or accessible through family doctors.

For all of this to work well, there would have to be good links between social, educational and health services, as well as good working relationships with employers. There would also need to be people within each of these areas of service who were familiar with the needs and problems of those with AS.

While good services for those with AS will not 'cure' their difficulties, they could help to reduce the impact of these difficulties on the lives of those with the condition and those around them. In such a situation, society might be much better placed to capitalize on the strengths of these unusual people rather than only noticing them when they cause problems. People with AS are not going to disappear. Indeed we are likely to become aware of more and more of them. They have probably always been around, but in the past we have seen them as the social outcasts and oddballs of society. In the twenty-first century, surely it is time to accept them as part of the human community with their own contribution to make, and to provide them with the necessary support to enable this to happen.

Summary

o   People with AS have a range of needs which current services do not meet effectively.

o   The following areas of need have been identified:

  •   social skills training and help in learning the rules of social situations

  •   advice and support to go out and meet others in a safe setting

  •   help to learn the necessary skills to get and keep a job

  •   advice and support in budgeting and managing money

  •   practical help and support with activities such as cooking, shopping and cleaning

  •   supported living opportunities which will give both independence and back-up.

o   Current services are poor and badly co-ordinated, and often rely on short-term research money or individual clinicians' special interests.

o   A range of adequately funded services is needed to meet the needs of those with different levels of ability. One size will not fit all.

o   Educational, social and health services need to be co-ordinated.

o   Good services will cost money, but might reduce existing costs by avoiding crises.

Further Reading

American Psychiatric Association (1994) *Diagnostic and Statistical Manual of Mental Disorders: Fourth Edition (DSM-IV)*. Washington, DC: American Psychiatric Association.

Asperger, H. (1944) `Die autischen psychopathen im kindesalter.' *Archiv fur Psychiatrie und Nervenkrankheiten, 117*, 76–137.

Attwood, T. (2008) *The Complete Guide to Asperger's Syndrome*. London: Jessica Kingsley Publishers.

Baron-Cohen, S. (2003) *The Essential Difference: Men, Women, and the Extreme Male Brain*. London: Allen Lane.

Department of Health (2001) *Valuing People: A New Strategy for Learning Disability for the 21st Century*. London: HMSO.

Ehlers, S., Nyden, A., Gillberg, C., Dahlgren Sandberg, A., Dahlgren, S.O., Hjelmquist, E. and Oden, A. (1997) 'Asperger Syndrome, Autism and Attentional Disorders: A comparative study of the cognitive profiles of 120 children.' *Journal of Child Psychology and Psychiatry, 37*, 207–217.

Ghaziuddin, M., Butler, L., Tsai, L. and Ghaziuddin, N. (1994) 'Is clumsiness a marker for Asperger Syndrome?' *Journal of Intellectual Disability Research, 38*, 519–527.

Gillberg, I.C. and Gillberg, C. (1989) 'Asperger Syndrome: Some epidemiological considerations. A research note.' *Journal of Child Psychology and Psychiatry, 30*, 631–638.

Howlin, P. (2000) 'Assessment instruments for Asperger Syndrome.' *Child Psychology and Psychiatry Review, 5*, 3, 120–129.

Klin, A., Volkmar, F.R. and Sparrow, S.S. (2000) *Asperger Syndrome*. New York: Guilford Publishers.

Leekam, S., Libby, S., Wing, L., Gould, J. and Gillberg, C. (2000) 'Comparison of ICD-10 and Gillberg's criteria for Asperger Syndrome.' *Autism: International Journal of Research and Practice, 4*, 11–28.

Macleod, A. (1999) 'Support scheme for adults with Asperger Syndrome.' *Autism, 3,* 2, 177–192.

Manjiviona, J. and Prior, M. (1995) 'Comparison of Asperger Syndrome and High-Functioning Autistic Children on a Test of Motor Impairment.' *Journal of Autism and Developmental Disorders, 25,* 23–29.

Miller, J.N. and Ozonoff, S. (1997) 'Did Asperger's cases have Asperger Disorder? A research note.' *Journal of Child Psychology and Psychiatry, 38,* 247–251.

Newson, E., Le Marechal, K. and David, C. (2003) 'Pathological demand avoidance syndrome: A necessary distinction within the pervasive developmental disorders.' *Archives of Disease in Childhood, 88,* 595–600.

Powell, A. (2002) *Taking Responsibility: Good practice guidelines for services – adults with Asperger syndrome.* London: The National Autistic Society.

Taylor, G. (1980) 'Adolescence and Early Adulthood (1): The Needs of the More Able Young Adults.' In K. Ellis (ed.) *Autism: Professional Perspectives and Practice.* London: Chapman and Hall.

Twachtman-Cullen, D. (1998) 'Language and Communication in High-Functioning Autism and Asperger Syndrome.' In E. Schopler, G. Mesibov and J. Kunce (eds) *Asperger Syndrome or High-Functioning Autism?* New York: Plenum Press.

Walker, D.R., Thompson, A., Zwaigenbaum, L., Goldberg, J., Bryson, S.E., Mahoney, W., Strawbridge, C.P. and Szatmiri, P. (2004) 'Specifying PDD-NOS: A comparison of PDD-NOS, Asperger Syndrome and Autism.' *Journal of American Academy of Child and Adolescent Psychiatry, 43,* 2, 172–180.

Weiss, M., Murray, C. And Weiss, G. (2002) 'Adults with Attention-Deficit/Hyperactivity Disorder: Current concepts.' *Journal of Psychiatric Practice, 8,* 2, 99–111.

Index